A SPACE FOR US

A GUIDE FOR LEADING BLACK, INDIGENOUS, AND PEOPLE OF COLOR AFFINITY GROUPS

MICHELLE CASSANDRA JOHNSON

T0243665

BEACON PRESS, BOSTON

BEACON PRESS
Boston, Massachusetts
www.beacon.org

Beacon Press books
are published under the auspices of
the Unitarian Universalist Association of Congregations.

26 25 24 23   8 7 6 5 4 3 2 1

This book is printed on acid-free paper that meets the uncoated paper
ANSI/NISO specifications for permanence as revised in 1992.

Text design and composition by Kim Arney

Excerpts from Kelsey Blackwell, "Why People of Color Need Spaces Without
White People," *The Arrow*, August 9, 2018; adrienne maree brown, *Holding Change:
The Way of Emergent Strategy Facilitation and Mediation* (Chico, CA: AK Press,
2021); Mia Mingus, "Dreaming Accountability," *Leaving Evidence* (blog), May
5, 2019, https://leavingevidence.wordpress.com; Naomi Ortiz, *Sustaining Spirit:
Self-Care for Social Justice* (Berkeley, CA: Reclamation Press, 2018); Gail Parker,
PhD, *Restorative Yoga for Ethnic and Race-Based Stress and Trauma* (London: Singing
Dragon, 2020), and kihana miraya ross, "Call It What It Is: Anti-Blackness,"
New York Times, June 4, 2020, are printed here with permission.

Names: Johnson, Michelle (Michelle Cassandra), author.
Title: A space for us : a guide for leading Black, indigenous, and people
of color affinity groups / Michelle Cassandra Johnson.
Description: Boston : Beacon Press, [2023] | Includes index. |
Summary: "The first comprehensive guide for leading BIPOC affinity
groups for challenging white supremacy, healing racial trauma,
and taking collective action"—Provided by publisher.
Identifiers: LCCN 2023014455 | ISBN 9780807007860 (trade paperback) |
ISBN 9780807007877 (ebook)
Subjects: LCSH: Anti-racism. | Racism—Prevention. | White
supremacy (Social structure) | Employee affinity groups.
Classification: LCC HT1563 .J64 2023 | DDC 305.8—dc23/eng/20230420
LC record available at https://lccn.loc.gov/2023014455

CONTENTS

FOREWORD

I HAD THE PLEASURE of meeting and sharing a co-facilitation role for a series of anti-racism workshops in 2018. Michelle and I both worked with white co-facilitators to lead these workshops. Meeting Michelle brought an incredible sense of solidarity, kinship, and relief!

Knowing that I would share this experience with Michelle, another Black woman who did not carry the normalized individualistic cultural expectations of white supremacy, I was excited.

Michelle's approach to working with white supremacy is deeply embodied and spiritual. Her incredible experience, rigorous analysis, and liberation practice was deep and present. At the time I was pregnant with my daughter and first child. My body was large, Black, woman, and pregnant. Being a Black pregnant facilitator was an embodied experience I had not expected. I realized almost daily that my body was not only taking up more space than normal, but that I had a body. And this body was holding the energy of racial trauma.

In the time that I shared this role with Michelle we must have held the hearts and spirits of thousands of bodies. While facilitating this workshop series my trauma response triggers came in response to the pain and dissociation that I witnessed in the experiences and lives of hundreds of people of color. At that time, we were holding space for racial affinity groups for all of the people of color who participated in our workshops. We were to make space for reflection and recovery for all of the employees who were BIPOC—Black, Indigenous, or People of Color. In many spaces the heartbreak of this racialized trauma is not allowed to take up space. These are the rules of white supremacy culture—the dominant culture of all institutions and life, unless it is named and worked with.

My work for many years prior to this experience followed an intellectual, robotic way of being. I learned to thwart my emotions to maintain emotional comfort. My internalized racial trauma was present and untended. I was not able to act out this emotionally avoidant survival skill in my pregnant body. The stakes were too high. I felt a level of hypervigilance that I had never known. This was a trauma response. My body was trying to play out an experience of historical, personal, or collective racial trauma.

Today, like Michelle, my liberation practice is steeped in embodied and spiritual ecology and practice. Michelle's voice is always with me, especially as I am actively engaged embodying skills that emerge from slow and conscious practice. When working with the body we can recognize the deep well of resources we can tap in to as a way to transmute the toxic embodied responses to white supremacy.

White supremacy is a system that works through the body. The body is weaponized through whiteness. For Black, Indigenous, and Bodies of Culture, white supremacy takes up all of the space until it is disrupted. It is relentless and persistent. As a culture it reproduces itself in all areas of social life and relationships. It claims dominion and ownership over spaces and bodies.

Resmaa Menakem, author of *My Grandmother's Hands: Mending the Wounds of Racialized Trauma*, says that the white body is the standard by which all bodies are measured, and any other body is a deviation from that norm. This puts the Black body at the greatest deviation from that standard. This structural and persistent institutional hierarchy places all people of color in opposition to themselves and each other. When asked why Bodies of Culture (people of color) need non-white spaces, Menakem says, "Racialized Spirit Murder is structural to white ferality and supremacy. It is not episodic. It is persistent. We must develop reprieve space to nurture our own emergence away from the white gaze."

The daily onslaught of pain is embodied as physical, psychological, psychic pain. It steals the dignity of Bodies of Culture. It leaves spiritual injuries from childhood that carry on through adult life and are passed down for generations through the expression of our DNA.

"Legal scholar Patricia Williams coined the term 'spirit murdering' to argue that racism is more than just physical pain; racism robs people of color of their humanity and dignity and leaves personal, psychological, and spiritual injuries. Racism is traumatic because it is a loss of protection, safety, nurturance, and acceptance—all things children need to enter school and learn," writes Bettina Love in *We Want to Do More Than Survive*.[1]

As a beekeeper and tender, Michelle's spirit is connected with cosmic pollinators. She has the awareness of the needs of the hearts and Bodies of Culture and color. She knows what medicine we need for healing. We need spaces where our bodies have the ability to settle from the threat of historical, intergenerational, and institutional violence. We need places to "re-member" ourselves, our dignity, and our sovereignty. We need spaces that allow for our testimony and sharing to be met with deep care—not to replay the story of trauma and remain stuck but to work with the body's inner well of resources, which allows us to metabolize the pain and move it out of the body. With this room in our nervous systems and our bodies' threat level lowered, we can retain culture, re-member our bodies and spirit. We need spaces for tender and slow grieving. We need spaces for telling our stories away from the white gaze. Spaces for healing the wounds of horizontal oppression that cause separation between people of color steeped in the waters of anti-Black racism. We need places to experience unconditional joy and love for ourselves. We need places to reclaim the cultural elements that have been stolen, lost, forgotten, and erased, including language, earth-honoring traditions, and ritual. A space for being and practicing soul-healing rituals.

I find healing possibilities and kinship with Michelle. Michelle is a guide and a holder of the spaces we need to reclaim our dignity and humanity.

—ERIN TRENT JOHNSON
Coach, facilitator, storyteller, and curator
of the Black.Mama.Body Experience

A SPACE
FOR US

MY FAVORITE PART

ATTENDED MY FIRST dismantling racism training in 1999. At the time, I was working as a clinical social worker at a high school and served on boards of directors of many nonprofits, including the North Carolina Lambda Youth Network. The organization sent all of its board members to dismantling racism training at a time when these trainings weren't readily available, social media blasts about performative allyship were nonexistent, and the collective consciousness about the insidiousness and horror of white supremacy and racism hadn't been raised via numerous videos of Black people being murdered by the police.

I arrived in Charleston, South Carolina, on a plantation where sixty people would gather over the course of a long weekend to deepen their understanding of personal, institutional, and cultural racism. It felt odd to be on a plantation while engaging in anti-racism work, and also interesting. The ghosts of my ancestors who were enslaved and their slave masters were with us mingling together as the truth about racism surfaced. I found myself in a room full of people—half of them were Black, Indigenous, and People of Color (BIPOC), mostly Black, and half white. Spiritual leaders, LGBTQIA+ activists, and community organizers gathered in a circle to work together and across lines of difference to create racial justice. I had come to this training as a Black woman who had grown up in Richmond, Virginia, attending private school and a predominantly white college. While I understood racism and never denied it was real or was happening to me, before entering the circle I didn't have the language to understand my experience of racism, nor a space to unpack how racism had impacted me so deeply and profoundly.

We sat in a circle, moved through different activities, developed a shared language, reviewed the History of the Race Construct, and had heated and generative discussions. At a certain point in the workshop, I found myself consoling a white woman who was crying because of her new realization: she was implicated in perpetuating white supremacy and racism. She felt guilty and confused. White supremacy had duped her, too, making her believe she was unique and special just because—not because of the fact that she benefited from white privilege and was afforded opportunities, wealth, access, and validation because of her whiteness. My humanness and compassionate nature were what guided me, and I didn't quite yet understand how my cultural conditioning and internalized racial oppression contributed to my caretaking role of her at the moment. One of the facilitators, Tema Okun, looked at me as I consoled the white woman and said to me, "She can take care of herself." Tema said this with firmness but care. I was a bit confused, and it took a little while for me to truly understand what was going on. Yes, part of my reaction stemmed from my compassionate heart, but part of it was definitely from the conditioned response that dominant culture and whiteness had taught me to take care of white people, protect their feelings, and make them feel comfortable.

As part of the training, we separated into groups by race. There was a white caucus and what was then called a People of Color (POC) caucus. When this idea was introduced to me immediately before we went to our caucuses, I was a bit uncomfortable. I didn't understand the purpose of separating, and I believe I was also wondering about how we would come back together. I knew we weren't having the same experience of living in a white supremacy culture, and I was confused about what we would talk about in a POC caucus that would be different than what would be talked about in the white caucus. I also sensed deep discomfort from some of the other participants—both white and BIPOC—in the training. So much of racial injustice comes from separation, isolation, othering, and division, yet we were asked to separate once again.

The group facilitator of the POC caucus, Bree, was a biracial woman who identified as Black. She opened our group by saying, "This is my favorite part of the training; it is wonderful to be here with you all." We proceeded to go around the circle for a check-in where each participant was invited to share how they were feeling. I don't know what I said when it was my turn. I have no recollection because I believe I was in deep study, investigating the makeup of our group, which included people from various racial and ethnic backgrounds, while listening to people's anger, sadness, and frustration about how systemic racism affected them.

The POC caucus was the first time the concept and experience of internalized racial oppression were introduced to me. It was defined as the way BIPOC people internalize negative messages from the dominant culture about being BIPOC. Self-doubt, self-hate, powerlessness, hopelessness, addiction, violence, and depression manifest as a result of internalization. It was further discussed as a manifestation of white supremacy and racism, which might cause BIPOC people to oppress themselves or other BIPOC people due to what dominant culture has taught them about who they are and what it means to be a BIPOC person. Last, it was discussed as the way BIPOC people perpetuate racial oppression against themselves and others, replicating the divide-and-conquer strategy of white supremacy, furthering a divide among BIPOC people, and in turn allowing white supremacy to thrive.

Upon my hearing this definition of internalized racial oppression, things started to click in place in my mind, body, heart, and spirit. I finally began to understand why I wore my hair straight, code-switched, and dressed the way I did. I understood why, when I saw other BIPOC people, I would at times have negative feelings toward them, or worse, blame them for their circumstances and suggest they could do better when in actuality they were up against a system designed to undo them. I understood why my mother sent me to a private school because she thought I would "get a better education." She sent me to this school and would also send me to places such as church camp or ballet class where Black people were the only people in attendance. I was made fun of time and time again in these spaces for "talking white," "dressing white," and "thinking I was white." I understood that I believed white was better because white supremacy had taught me so and made me believe assimilation was the answer.

While holding these things in my mind, as puzzle pieces started to come together and click into place, I also knew that injustice was real and that whole groups of people were discriminated against for identities they embodied. I knew that I had been discriminated against for my race by white people. I was aware that there wasn't a level playing field, and I was angry at how BIPOC people were treated. I knew I had a role and work to do to fight oppression, and I was committed to making change in my community and beyond. The duality of sitting with how I had perpetuated racial oppression against other BIPOC people and myself and being committed to fighting for racial justice created dissonance inside me. I sat in the POC caucus with a lot of questions about how I had been conditioned and trained to be as a Black person by culture, my mother and family, my white friends, my white partner, and the Black children I grew up with who would make fun of me because I didn't fit the stereotypical image of what it meant to be Black. The experience of being in the POC caucus left me feeling curious about the work I, and we as BIPOC people, needed to do to heal the wounds and scars created by white supremacy and internalized racial oppression.

After meeting in our caucuses, and later on that evening, we gathered together again as one large group for cultural sharing, which was quite a cultural experiment. The LGBTQIA+ activists shared about their work while Black faith leaders shared how they were faced with the dynamics of intersectionality and things that made them feel quite uncomfortable. I saw sexual orientation and gender identity bump up against whiteness and racism. The white women's rights activists were faced with anger from Black women elders in the group because it was difficult for the activists to hold racism and sexism at the same time while Black women had compounded oppressed identities by being Black and women. This experience raised questions about how we work across various lines of difference and maintain our shared humanity. Over the course of the weekend, I learned not only about white supremacy and racism but also about what we internalize from the dominant culture about who we are, and I learned about the harm that this causes to us as individuals and to the collective. I left the training feeling excited and eager to share what I had learned with my partner, friends, and coworkers. I went back to work on Monday feeling like a layer of who I was had been exposed because I understood more about who I was in terms of race. I forgot that the rest of the faculty at the high school had not attended the workshop and therefore hadn't had the same experience. It felt disjointed to want to share new information about the world, white supremacy, and racism while not having a place to share it.

Time passed and I noticed that the curiosity I continued to experience about the training was significant; I felt compelled to learn more from the facilitators about how to become a dismantling racism trainer. I followed up with Tema and Bree. I met with Tema in Durham, North Carolina, and we talked about what it might be like for me to "train up" as a dismantling racism trainer. After my meeting with Tema, she introduced me to Kenneth Jones, another trainer and the cofounder of Changeworks, an organization that led anti-racism trainings in communities and organizations. Kenneth's fire, passion, and humor sold me on becoming a dismantling racism trainer.

For a couple of years, I attended countless dismantling racism trainings—observing, taking notes, and learning about facilitation in emotionally charged places. I sat in caucuses and witnessed what it was like to come back together as a large group after having been separated by race. I facilitated sections of the training curriculum and after a while was able to co-facilitate with our team of trainers.

I remember the first time I co-led a POC caucus with Kenneth. Bree's words came back to me: "This is my favorite part of the training." At that moment, I offered these same words to the group. I understood that as BIPOC people we were on the receiving end of racism and were living in a culture that was hell-bent on annihilating us because of our race. I understood how whiteness could suck the air out of the room and center itself instead of caring for the people who have been most harmed by racism—BIPOC people. I understood why we needed a place to cry, scream, and heal. It all became clear to me, and from that point on, my favorite part of each training was the POC caucus. Even as a facilitator, it was the space I went to for healing and validation.

I've been learning about and leading dismantling racism work since 1999. I have worked in organizations, corporations, and communities, chipping away at white supremacy and its wrath. I understand white supremacy and its most effective strategy: divide and conquer. I have experienced BIPOC and white people taking collective action in spite of white supremacy and racism, in spite of internalized racial superiority and oppression.

I have facilitated countless BIPOC caucuses holding people's hearts as they try to unravel the toxicity white supremacy breeds. I've worked through moments of conflict and growth in caucuses. I have sat in my own space of inferiority and doubt due to what white supremacy says about who I am, and I have remembered who I truly am—a whole, divine, beautiful being, committed to collective action and our collective liberation.

The need for a resource and guide to support BIPOC in sharing space together and centering their own healing is long overdue. *A Space for Us: A Guide for Leading Black, Indigenous, and People of Color Affinity Groups* is vital and necessary as we navigate the resurgence of the Black Lives Matter movement while white-bodied people try to figure out their right role in interrupting and dismantling racism. We continue to need spaces to heal and be as we are. We need spaces to witness one another and call each other in when internalized racial oppression has made us forget who we are.

I wrote this book from my experience as a Black person and someone who is at the bottom of the racial hierarchy . If you are biracial or mixed roots, please know that some of what I offer in this book may resonate and some of it may not. Depending on your lived experience and proximity to whiteness, you may also choose to read a complementary resource focused on leading affinity groups for folks who identify as biracial or mixed roots.

If you are more proximal to white and hence to social and institutional power because of your skin tone, or if more often than not people assume you are white (sometimes referred to as white-passing), please read these words with an understanding that your experience as someone who is more proximal to power—because of the ability you have to pass as white if you choose—is different from my identity as a Black person. Because of my skin tone, there is no question that I am Black, which means I am racialized in all settings and all of the time. Because I do not have the lived experience of being able to pass as white and as a Black person I am not adjacent to white in the racial hierarchy, I understand that my experience as a Black person is vastly different from your experience. I ask you to consider if you are the right person to lead a BIPOC affinity group; if you feel it is aligned for you to lead this kind of space, consider how you will speak to your identity in a BIPOC group. Later, I will share about how to hold space and facilitate, and I will share about holding a BIPOC space versus holding a space for a specific racial identity or ethnicity.

If you are white and have chosen to read this book, I invite you to ask yourself why you have chosen to read it. If your reason feels aligned with values and principles rooted in dismantling racism, then you might choose to continue reading. Please remember that I wrote *A Space for Us* for a BIPOC audience and from my experience of being Black. I didn't write this for white-bodied people. If you are white, there are books and resources available for you to learn more about whiteness and how to hold space for other white-bodied people. *A Space for Us* is not one of these resources. I wrote this book for BIPOC people. We need a space for our own healing that isn't shrouded by whiteness, white-bodied people, and white supremacy.

This guide is an offering from me to BIPOC people who want to work together for our sovereignty and liberation. The guide does not contain all of the answers. It does include tools, resources, validation, and a framework to better understand what white supremacy is doing to us as BIPOC people and in turn what we are doing to one another. It is a guide that my heart hopes is useful to many and helps us illuminate the pathway to freedom.

A Space for Us includes wisdom from some amazing BIPOC space-holders and facilitators. The appendix includes biographical information and ways to connect with the people I interviewed for *A Space for Us* along with additional resources to support you.

CHAPTER 1

WHITE SUPREMACY, RACISM, AND THE FOUR FOUNDATIONS

If now isn't a good time for the truth, I don't see when we'll get to it.
—NIKKI GIOVANNI

WHEN I WAS a child, and as I grew up, I didn't observe phrases like "structural racism" and "white supremacy" being used in the mainstream. I never heard these terms on the news, saw them on the cover or in magazines, or experienced them being brought up in casual conversation. When someone would mention these terms, it almost felt like the experience of hearing a whisper about a recent cancer diagnosis, as if whispering was going to dampen the intensity of one's illness. Throughout time, I learned that whispering didn't make cancer, racism, or white supremacy cease to be. Whispering about systems that are embedded in the foundation of how the US came to be has exacerbated the idea that racism and white supremacy are taboo things to discuss and are meant to be hidden instead of acknowledged. Whispering functions as a tool of dominance and supremacy; we've whispered for long enough. White supremacy and racism are realities that affect us all. These systems of dominance and superiority have been seeded into the soil and have flourished over many, many years. It is time for us to dig and turn the soil so that white supremacy and racism are not buried further into the layers of the earth. It is time for us to understand the toxic nature of white supremacy and racism, and it is time for us to deepen our understanding of how these toxins impact us as BIPOC people.

Many years ago, a mentor of mine shared with me the steps one can take to raise consciousness and deepen understanding of a problem: develop a shared language so you understand what you are talking about, develop a shared understanding of an analysis of the problem so you can strategize to interrupt, intervene, disrupt, dismantle it, and heal from the trauma the problem may be causing, and do not expect the problem to go away because you've engaged in one consciousness-raising opportunity. This wisdom has served me well in my more than two decades of leading anti-racism work. Shared language and analysis are the way I level-set or as I lead people through a consciousness-raising process. It is where we will begin as well.

Before we explore shared language and analysis focused on white supremacy and racism, it feels important for me to share an assumption about the way I approach the transformative work of dismantling racism. I will share a more complete list of assumptions later in the chapter. This is a book intended for BIPOC who are interested in healing and holding space for other BIPOC to heal in community with one another. Given that you are most likely a BIPOC person reading and engaging the resources and tools offered throughout *A Space for Us*, I want to name this reality: As BIPOC people, we often have a clear understanding of white supremacy culture—we have to navigate this culture at every turn. We are conditioned and socialized to see and experience ourselves as racialized beings, and often white-bodied people are conditioned to see themselves as the norm rather than as racialized.

In this section, I want to share my understanding of racism and white supremacy, because if you are planning to lead or participate in a BIPOC affinity group, it is important to have a shared understanding and analysis of racism. In affinity spaces, we are responding to white supremacy culture—the wounds it causes and the wounds it causes us to inflict upon each other. In affinity spaces, we seek pathways to healing from the fragmentation we may feel because white supremacy conditions most of us to think of ourselves as inferior and less than. I want to take the time to level-set here so you have a clear understanding of how we came to be in a time and space where we need to meet in affinity groups in order to heal our spirits, in order to take collective action to dismantle racism, and, if we choose, to work across communities of difference.

SHARED LANGUAGE

When someone is brave or provocative enough to name the ever-present elephant in the room—white supremacy and racism—white supremacy does one of two things: either there is an attempt to deny its existence, or it gets louder through what can feel like passive or explicit aggressive actions and confusing patterns of whiteness meant to silence whoever unearthed and spoke the truth. Words like "white supremacy" and "racism" can feel emotionally charged for BIPOC and white-bodied people. These systems *are* charged, and it makes sense why we would feel emotional about them.

I was born in 1975 and grew up thinking racism was about refusing to tolerate those who embodied different identities than me and having prejudice rather than an intentional system meant to classify and assign value to certain groups while devaluing others, dividing and conquering us. In my own family, we spoke about race without using the terms "racism" or "white supremacy." As I attended a predominantly white school, which was most certainly founded on racist values and principles, I never once learned about racism through a teacher's curriculum. I learned about racism through the teacher's actions, which were implicit to them and explicit to me. In large part, so many of us have been conditioned to misunderstand what "racism" and "white supremacy" mean.

When I attended my first dismantling racism training at age twenty-three, I was introduced to the concept of shared language. The process of creating shared language was like how a cool spring feels on one's skin on a hot day—I found it refreshing. I was thrilled someone was telling the truth about what we as BIPOC people felt and experienced. Since that time, I have prioritized being clear about terms and what we are talking about when we use them, especially if we are building strategies with others to dismantle systems of power that only serve a small few and oppress many.

Many of the definitions of terms given in this section are informed by my involvement with Dismantling Racism Works (dRworks), a training collective of which I was a member for over two decades. These definitions are also influenced by critical race theory, feminist theory, and my own experience and understanding of these concepts.

ABOLITIONISM The act of abolishing an oppressive system. Abolitionism purports that we cannot end oppression by replicating more oppressive structures; a core principle of abolitionism is our shared humanity.

BLOOD MEMORIES I first heard this term from my friend and colleague Vivette Jeffries-Logan. I heard her share it in the context of a Dismantling Racism workshop that we were co-facilitating. She was sharing about the generational and ancestral trauma she embodies as an Indigenous woman because of white supremacy, which tried to annihilate and force her ancestors to assimilate through a violent process of erasing Indigenous culture. She called these blood memories. As I heard Vivette speak about blood memories, it made me think about epigenetics and how trauma is passed on from one generation to the next. Memories are passed on not just verbally but through genetic memory and code. As I understand it, Indigenous elders often talk about memory being contained in the blood and bones. To me, this speaks to the ancestral trauma and resilience that can be passed on through blood and bone given that we are made manifest because of our ancestors. These memories and the ancestral patterns that emerge in us from our bloodlines may show up unconsciously, and the idea is that we cannot extract memory from the blood and bone. Our memory is bone-deep. In affinity spaces, often we are responding to blood memories. We as facilitators are holding these memories while creating the potential for healing that needs to occur in relationship to them.

COLLECTIVE GRIEF Grief felt by the collective in response to loss that affects us all such as war, a pandemic, or systemic oppression. We as BIPOC people are carrying grief in our bodies, cells, and tissues from the history of systemic racism that lives in our bodies from our ancestors and their experience of living in a white supremacy culture. This ancestral grief is compounded by our own experience of loss due to structures like white supremacy. Although as BIPOC people we may have experienced different losses because of white supremacy culture, there is a commonality between them because of how systemic racism operates.

COLONIALISM An ideology advocating for the acquisition or colonization of other people's property, or of other people and their culture.

CULTURAL APPROPRIATION Taking or adopting one or more elements from one culture without an appreciation for or a relationship with that culture. The people taking the elements from a culture with which they are not connected are often in the dominant position or represent the dominant culture. There is usually material, emotional, physical, or spiritual gain for the person or people engaging in cultural appropriation. In other words, dominant culture profits from cultural appropriation, which causes material, emotional, physical, and spiritual suffering for people marginalized by dominant culture.

CULTURAL TRAUMA Dysregulation of a collective's nervous system often due to systemic oppression or as a response to tragic and horrific events that forever shift a group of people's consciousness and identity. Cultural trauma is the experience of disruption on a collective scale.

CULTURE Norms, standards, beliefs, values, and narratives created by a particular nation, people, or social group.

DISCRIMINATION Action based on prejudice. Discrimination is always happening. There is no prejudice without discrimination because how we see the world drives our actions.

DOMINANT CULTURE A system that inherently believes some people are superior and others, inferior. This system of dominance and inferiority is based on various identities such as race, gender and gender expression, age, physical or mental capabilities, and sexual orientation (this list is not comprehensive, as we hold many other identities beyond those mentioned here). Dominant culture creates norms that determine who is "normal." When one is seen as "normal" based on their identities, they are positioned to be in closer proximity to social and institutional power. Therefore, dominant culture functions as a gatekeeper by deciding who has access to power and, furthermore, access to move with ease as they navigate their life.

ETHNICITY The terms "ethnicity" and "race" are often confused and conflated. As shared in the definition of race, race was constructed, has changed over time, and was set up as a hierarchy. Ethnicity is often connected to geography or a culture's place or origin. For example, the construct of race defines me as Black while my ethnicity is actually 80 percent West African—specifically, Nigerian—and 20 percent Irish. Things such as dance, language, food, customs, traditions, dress, and so forth are often connected to culture and one's ethnicity.

HARM Harm means many things, and the way we talk about it is often determined by the context, who we perceive to have caused harm or hurt, and whom we perceive as having experienced harm, along with power dynamics and the influence of dominant culture in a specific context. When I refer to "harm" in this book, and in dismantling racism and anti-oppression trainings and in healing and liberatory work, I always connect it with systems and systemic oppression. Many of the harms caused by oppression haven't been fully acknowledged or accounted for through reparations or other models of restorative justice. For example, the History of the Race Construct is not taught widely in our educational system. Those of us who are descendants of enslaved peoples have not been positioned to make decisions about what repair and healing we might need as a result of the violent acts of oppression we have experienced at the hands of white supremacy. As a group, white people haven't taken responsibility for what their internalized white supremacy breeds. For example, Indigenous people continue to have to fight for their sovereignty. Dominant culture has set up systems determined to divide us from ourselves and from one another, and to make us act from a place of believing we are fragmented instead whole. These systems deeply influence how we relate to one another, whether or not we feel accountable to one another, and how we navigate through the world. Not feeling that we are whole and connected to one another and the planet creates an immense amount of trauma and pain; when we do not work to understand our positionality and social location based on where culture assigns us power and how we affect others, we risk replicating what dominant culture does—we create conditions for harm to happen instead of conditions for liberation. It is my understanding and experience that harm has interrupted our ability to heal individually and collectively—harm such as white fragility, police brutality, entitlement, defensiveness, colonization, cultural appropriation, cis-hetero-patriarchy, ableism, ageism, classism, sizeism, and other forms of oppression. We are all harmed by dominant culture, and harmed in different ways, and we have our own individual experiences of trauma and times when we have experienced harm.

IMPLICIT BIAS Also known as implicit social cognition, implicit bias refers to the attitudes or stereotypes that affect our understanding, actions, and decisions in an unconscious manner. These biases, which encompass both favorable and unfavorable assessments, are activated involuntarily and without an individual's awareness or intentional control. Residing deep in the subconscious, these biases are different from known biases that individuals may choose to conceal for the purposes of social or political correctness. Unlike known biases, implicit biases are not accessible through introspection.

An example of implicit bias would be when an American citizen assumes that someone who has accent that sounds foreign doesn't speak English, or "good English," so the American citizen speaks very loudly to the person who has an accent. Another example of implicit bias is the assumption that all Black people are good at sports. This assumption could cause an educator to encourage a student to play sports like basketball or football instead of focusing on classroom studies. One more example of implicit bias is the assumption that elders age sixty-five and older have limited cognitive abilities. This could lead someone younger than sixty-five to speak loudly to an elder when explaining something or, worse, to assume that an elder doesn't understand what is being communicated to them.

INDIVIDUALISM Belief systems that uphold the interests of the individual as paramount to the interests of the collective.

INTERNALIZED RACISM A multigenerational process of dehumanization where People of Color internalize feelings of inferiority and white people internalize feelings of superiority.

INTERSECTIONALITY A term coined by Kimberlé Crenshaw and an idea first centered by Sojourner Truth, intersectionality asks us to consider all the identities we embody—the ones assigned privilege and the ones experiencing oppression due to culture's construction of identities and the value or lack of value it places on them.[1] Intersectionality asks us to look at the intersection of our identities to better understand how we navigate the world and how we work across lines of difference. For example, I am a Black, able-bodied, middle-class, cisgender, heterosexual woman.

LIVING ANCESTOR This is a concept first introduced to me by Layla Saad, the author of *Me and White Supremacy*. Layla hosts a podcast called *Good Ancestor*, where she explores what it means to be a good ancestor with her guests. The premise is that we are supported by our ancestors who have transitioned, and we are living ancestors, deciding what our legacy will be with our actions, intentions, beliefs, and the ways we express our values and what we value. Saad writes, "The Good Ancestor understands the both/and of their limitations as human beings, and the infiniteness of the legacy they can create and leave for others *if* they choose to focus on what they can do consistently with depth, vigour and even joy."[2]

My friend and colleague Stephanie Ghoston Paul has also created a podcast, *Take Nothing When I Die*, which is an exploration of what it means to be a living ancestor. Stephanie focuses on the dreams we can manifest, the words we can say, and the actions we can take now instead of taking them to the graveyard with us after we transition. So many people's dreams, inventions, wishes, hopes, and desires live in the graveyard or wherever you believe a person goes after they leave their physical body. Being a living ancestor is about bringing our dreams, inventions, wishes, hopes, and desires to fruition now so that we and the future generations can benefit from them.

OPPRESSION The subjugation of one group of people to elevate another group of people. Often it involves violence but isn't limited to physical violence. It can include emotional, mental, spiritual, and psychic violence as well.

"OPPRESSION TAKES THE BREATH AWAY" This is an expression I first spoke in July 2014 after the murder of Eric Garner. I watched the video of his murder, went to teach a noon yoga class, and spoke these words for the first time: "We live in a culture where oppression takes the breath away." It does so physically by taking away someone's capacity to breathe, emotionally by causing great suffering through the act of oppression and subjugation, mentally by causing anxiety, PTSD (post-traumatic stress disorder), depression, and grief, and spiritually by trying to extinguish one's life force.

PRIVILEGE Societal benefits bestowed upon people socially, politically, and economically. Privilege can be based on race, class, age, ability level, mental health status, gender, sexual orientation, and sex assigned at birth.

RACE A socially constructed system of classifying humans based on phenotypical characteristics (skin color, hair texture, bone structure). There is no scientific or biological evidence for race, yet the perception of race is *real* and remains a powerful political, social, and economic force. Race is essentially a political construct; in other words, it was constructed for political purposes. The term "white" was constructed to unite certain European groups living in the US who were fighting each other and at the same time were a numerical minority in comparison to the numbers of African slaves and Native peoples. In order to justify the idea of a white race, every institution in this country was used to prove that race exists and to promote the idea that the white race is at the top and all other races are below, with the Black race on the bottom. All institutions were used to promote the idea of white supremacy.

RACISM Racism manifests from the social construction of race. It happens not only on a personal level, but it also deeply influences our interpersonal relationships across difference based on race and other identities, affects how institutions are structured and function, and has shaped cultural norms and what or who is seen as normal. In this way, racism occurs on many levels.

Racism is racial prejudice plus social and institutional power. Racism is prejudice based on race, which we all can embody and act upon, backed up by social and institutional power, the ability to influence who is resourced and who is not, and to make policy decisions that affect us all but affect us differently, depending on our racial identity. Racism derived from a social and political structure that deemed white as superior and being BIPOC as inferior.

Racism is advantage based on race. White-bodied people are advantaged financially, emotionally, physically, psychically, spiritually, and mentally because of their white skin, which positions them in closer proximity to social and institutional power.

Racism is oppression based on race. BIPOC people experience oppression financially, emotionally, physically, psychically, emotionally, spiritually, and mentally, because of how the racial hierarchy was constructed with white at the top and anyone who is BIPOC below white.

Racism is a white supremacy system. Racism is a system in which people inherently believe white is superior.

RITUAL Often defined as a set of actions we perform consistently and in a prescribed manner. I have a morning ritual: getting out of bed, brushing my teeth, taking my medication, and making lemon water with honey. There are rituals I participate in that are infused with Spirit such as prayer, meditation, new moon and full moon ceremonies, and solstice and equinox celebrations. Meeting in affinity groups is also a ritual—a ritual designed to provide healing spaces specifically for BIPOC people and white folks to heal and remember. As I write about rituals in *A Space for Us*, I am writing about rituals that are a set of actions performed in an effort to remind us of our wholeness and create liberation for us, as BIPOC people, to be free.

SOCIAL AND INSTITUTIONAL POWER The power wielded by entities like governments, churches, and corporations to control people and direct their behavior through access to resources, the ability to influence others, access to decision-makers to get what you want done, and the ability to define reality for yourself and others.

SOCIAL LOCATION Social location refers to social group membership and identities. It is a tool used to reflect on the groups that people belong to because of their place or position in history and society. It is a tool used to allow people to clearly identify their proximity to power based on the identities they embody. Everyone has a social location that is defined by race, gender, gender expression, social class, age, ability level, sexual orientation, geographic location, and context.

SPIRIT I do not believe there is a way for us to heal our hearts without recognizing our inherent humanity and divinity. I bring the spirit and Spirit into my work to support healing on all levels. I know my ancestors believed in something bigger than themselves, and this is part of what allowed them to survive the unfathomable conditions of the system of slavery. If you are someone who does not have a spiritual connection or faith tradition, the content in this book will still be useful.

I share about Spirit here so that when I reference Spirit in different sections of this book, you have a clear understanding of what I mean and am referencing. I conceptualize Spirit as a power and energy that is much larger than me and contained inside me. Spirit can be felt through the elements—air, water, on the earth, in the heavens, in our bodies, and around us. People use different words to describe Spirit, including God, Father, Divine, Mother, Creator, and so on. Spirit is an energy from whom I seek guidance and support. I pray to Spirit and my spirit guides each day. Spirit guides are energies in the spiritual world, not the material world; spirit guides are positive in nature and offer assistance to me in various ways.

Spirit guides are sometimes referred to as angels, archangels, guardians, elemental energies, and ancestors.

TRANSFORMATION Transformation is about changing something from one state into another. It can feel complicated to change, and it can also feel comforting. The work we do—anti-oppression, liberation, dismantling racism—enables us to come into our humanity, heal ourselves, and create healing pathways for and with others. This is transformative in nature because it calls us into noticing where we are out of alignment with our values and principles, shift paradigms, and be open to changing our perspective or to discovering something new; something we previously didn't know or see. This kind of transformative work calls us into observing all the ways we have moved away from humanity and invites—or at times challenges—us to come back into wholeness and alignment with one another and the planet.

TRAUMA There are many types of trauma, and I explain more about trauma throughout *A Space for Us*. For the purposes of understanding trauma now and developing a shared understanding, I define trauma as a disruption of and shock to the nervous system. Trauma occurs when something happens to us that we didn't expect. Something that we perceive as not normal and something we must work to integrate as part of our experience in order to heal. Trauma is an experience that causes one person or a group of people to move out of balance. The shock of continually being taught one is inferior or of fearing for one's life because of one's race, and the hypervigilance and the physical, mental, and emotional stress that manifests from this kind of shock is what we call racial trauma. It is often an experience that is not within one's control. Often one has to engage healing modalities such as therapy, movement, energy work, journaling, yoga, pranayama, meditation, ceremony, and ritual to bring the nervous system back into homeostasis.

WHITE SUPREMACY The idea (ideology) that white people and the ideas, thoughts, beliefs, and actions of white people are superior to People of Color and their ideas, thoughts, beliefs, and actions. While most people associate white supremacy with extremist groups like the Ku Klux Klan and neo-Nazis, white supremacy is ever-present in our institutional and cultural assumptions that assign value, morality, goodness, and humanity to the white group while casting people and communities of color as worthless (worth less), immoral, bad, inhuman, and "undeserving." Drawing on critical race theory, the term "white supremacy" also refers to a political or socioeconomic system where white people enjoy structural advantages and rights that other racial and ethnic groups do not, at both a collective and an individual level.

You will see these terms throughout *A Space for Us* and while you do not have to agree with my definition of the terms previously listed, they are listed here so you better understand my point of reference and perspective.

ASSUMPTIONS

In addition to shared language, I would like to offer a more complete list of assumptions that I bring to this work. These assumptions inform how I lead BIPOC affinity spaces and may be a tool you want to use as you facilitate your own BIPOC affinity groups.

Earlier in the chapter, I shared an assumption about our experience as BIPOC and how many of us have been conditioned to see ourselves as racialized beings, while the white supremacy culture conditions white-bodied people to see themselves as the norm and not as racialized beings. Here I offer more assumptions, which speak to what informs my experience as a Black person and anti-racism educator and activist, as well as the philosophy and belief system I hold in my anti-racism work. Many of these assumptions derive from a collaboration with my colleagues at Dismantling Racism Works. Some of the assumptions come from my work with my colleague, Kerri Kelly, in our collaborative work, the organization Race and Resilience. Many social justice activists and magnificent space-holders have put their energy into formulating these assumptions:

- We live in a toxic culture that affects us all. We are not encouraged to see it, so we must learn to see our culture and how it teaches us to transform the absurd into normal.
- Intent is not the same as impact. We need to understand that we can have good intentions and still have a hurtful or damaging impact.
- Analyzing and cultivating awareness is a lifelong process. We all have questions. I hope to address some of your questions

throughout the book, and my hope and assumption is that once you complete this book, you will have more questions at a deeper level.

- There is no way to talk about racism without the risk of replicating it.
- We have to develop awareness of ourselves, of our communities, and of the world—both as individuals and in community. We have to work together to love ourselves into who we want to be.
- We have to believe in the possibilities of creating the world we want to see by aligning our actions with our values and learning from our mistakes.
- We are interconnected and interdependent.
- Our well-being is inextricably bound with that of others.
- None of this is easy and we have to do it anyway.
- We are not broken. Dominant culture and capitalism want us to believe that if we consume or purchase certain things we will feel whole. These systems (which are most definitely not designed for us to remember our wholeness) rest on an assumption we are broken and need to be fixed. Many things do need to be repaired in our world, but we are not broken. We are whole, and part of our work toward collective liberation is remembering our collective wholeness and remembering that we are interconnected with every other living being and with the planet.

A FURTHER NOTE ON LANGUAGE

I want to offer one more bit of information about language: it changes all of the time. Language shift is an indication that culture is evolving in some way. For example, when I first began leading anti-racism work, we used the term "People of Color" (POC) instead of BIPOC (Black, Indigenous, and People of Color). Some people use the term "Bodies of Culture" or "People of the Global Majority" to describe Black and Brown folks across the globe. (The term "Body of Culture" was coined by Resmaa Menakem, author of *My Grandmother's Hands: Racialized Trauma and the Pathway to Mending Our Hearts and Bodies*.) Unlike when I was a child, I hear "white supremacy" on the news, read it on social media, and hear it often in the spaces in which I lead and move. People who attend your BIPOC affinity spaces will have different understandings of language and different orientations to the terms and their meanings. Please know that the terms offered in the previous section are the ones I use, and I am fully aware that you may have different terms to describe the same concepts, and these terms may change tomorrow, next week, next year, or within the next decade.

THE THREE EXPRESSIONS OF RACISM

In addition to discussing language, I want to share a brief framework about personal, institutional, and cultural racism. This is also part of level-setting and is meant to support you in developing a better understanding of the cultural and political context in which we currently exist. Many people who attend your BIPOC affinity group are affected personally by racism and internalized oppression, working in or interacting with institutions, and living within a culture that uplifts whiteness and devalues and oppresses BIPOC people. This framework will further clarify the definition of racism from the "Shared Language" section of this chapter. The framework I share here is deeply informed by my work with dRworks and my experience of facilitating anti-racism work. Some people who work within the field of racial equity include the interpersonal level in the framework. I will speak to it and focus on the three levels identified earlier—personal, institutional, and cultural racism.

To assist in developing a better understanding of the power analysis, the diagram in figure 1.1 illustrates the three different levels of racism.

Personal Racism

The diagram in figure 1.1 is a person who represents every person— BIPOC, white-bodied, mixed roots, or biracial. The person is a representation of personal racism, which is often expressed as implicit or unconscious bias. As Charlotte Ruhl, a researcher of implicit social cognition, notes, "An implicit bias may run counter to a person's conscious beliefs without them realizing it. For example, it is possible to express explicit liking of a certain social group or approval of a certain action, while simultaneously being biased against that group or action on an unconscious level."[3]

We are shaped and influenced by our socialization, which includes the systems we are born into or inherit, the environment in which we live and grow up, our interactions with institutions and cultural norms, and

FIGURE 1.1

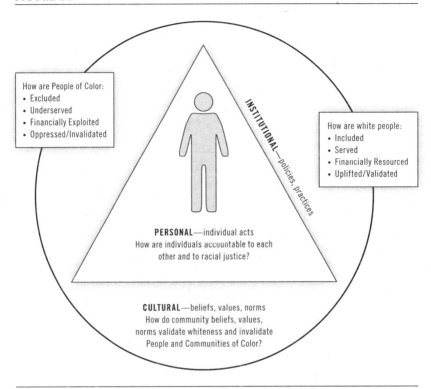

How are People of Color:
• Excluded
• Underserved
• Financially Exploited
• Oppressed/Invalidated

INSTITUTIONAL—policies, practices

How are white people:
• Included
• Served
• Financially Resourced
• Uplifted/Validated

PERSONAL—individual acts
How are individuals accountable to each
other and to racial justice?

CULTURAL—beliefs, values, norms
How do community beliefs, values,
norms validate whiteness and invalidate
People and Communities of Color?

what we learn about incentives to uphold the status quo and systems of
dominance and superiority versus challenging and breaking down systems
of dominance and superiority. Our shaping affects our beliefs and the
biases we hold consciously and unconsciously. Our biases affect how we
interact with others and view ourselves and the world. "Personal racism
is the ways in which white-bodied people, because of their internalized
sense of superiority and biases supported by institutions and dominant
cultural norms, perpetuate and/or assume the idea that white people are
inherently better and/or BIPOC communities and people are inherently
inferior on an individual basis. Examples: calling someone a racist name,
making a racist assumption."[4] When we as BIPOC people express bias
toward white-bodied people, we are expressing prejudice, not racism. For
an action to be racist, it must be enacted by a group who has been supported by social and institutional power. Throughout history and because
of colonialism and colonization and the creation of a racial hierarchy and

white supremacy, BIPOC people have not been backed up by or supported by social and institutional power. This is important to understand because at times some BIPOC people will come into your affinity space confused about the definition of racism and about how social and institutional power operate. The definition of racism and personal racism coupled with this framework can offer some clarity, relief, and a sense of liberation for a BIPOC person who has been taught through socialization to believe in things like reverse racism.

Institutional Racism

The next part of the analysis is the triangle, which represents institutional racism. As noted in the diagram, institutional racism is often enacted through policies, practices, protocols, and the ways these things negatively affect BIPOC people disparately. When I consider the different institutions my ancestors and I have interacted with throughout history, there is a common thread: as Black people we have been excluded, underserved, exploited, and oppressed. We have been denied access to certain spaces, been locked out of rooms where policies are made, and silenced through a process of not inviting us to a seat at the table.

> "A seat at the table means you are part of the conversation."
> —ROXANE GAY, "What a 'Seat at the Table' Means in the Black Lives Matter Era,"
> *Seat at the Table* podcast, October 14, 2020 *CBC Podcasts*

And if we aren't part of the conversation, decisions will be made for and about us that are not in our best interest but are instead in the interest of upholding white supremacy. Institutions such as education, housing, banking, criminal justice, and commerce have been set up to underserve BIPOC people. While policies have been put in place to level the playing field, inequity still exists because there has never been an accounting for why the field wasn't level to begin with, and there has never been a reparations process. Our needs have been silenced and ignored over and over by institutions. Institutions have exploited our bodies and minds. Our bodies have been used for labor, and the fruits of this labor were never seen by us as BIPOC people but instead were pocketed by white hands and systems designed to uphold the idea that white is superior. Our knowledge has been taken from us and our minds have been mined for their brilliance.

Institutions have a historical pattern of oppressing communities of color. We have been subjugated to violence and denial of care due to policies or a lack thereof. Institutions have worked to silence our voices when we speak up about racist practices and protocols. We have been locked out and kicked out of institutions. We have also been asked to assimilate into institutions, which so often are not set up to care for us but instead to condition us to go along to get along in spaces where conditions do not exist for us to thrive.

As a BIPOC person, I invite you to consider how you have experienced these types of behaviors as you have been a part of or interacted with different institutions such as health care, housing, banking, nonprofit organizations, social services, local government, and so forth.

- When and how have you experienced exclusion? When and how have you experienced being underserved, exploited, and oppressed?
- What examples of these behaviors have you witnessed happening to others?
- How did these experiences make you feel?

The definition of institutional racism used by Dismantling Racism Works and many other groups working to dismantle institutional and structural racism is

the ways in which the structures, systems, policies, and procedures of institutions in the U.S. are founded upon and then promote, reproduce, and perpetuate advantages for white people and the oppression of BI- POC communities and people. The ways in which institutions legislate and structure reality to advantage white people and oppress BIPOC communities and people. The ways in which institutions—Housing, Government, Education, Media, Business, Health Care, Criminal Justice, Employment, Labor, Politics, Church—perpetuate racism. Examples: BIPOC communities and people underrepresented and misrepresented on television[;] racially-biased standardized tests used to determine who will be admitted to higher education programs and institutions[;] historic and ongoing breaking of treaties with indigenous Native American communities[;] reliance on low-paying undocumented immigrant labor by farms and factories.[5]

Institutional racism works in concert with cultural racism, which is the next level of the analysis about the three expressions of racism.

Cultural Racism

Cultural racism is represented by the circle in the diagram in figure 1.1 and encloses the triangle and person. Several racial equity scholars and educators describe culture as the air we breathe and the water we swim in. This speaks to the reality that culture is all-encompassing. It is around us and influences our thoughts, behaviors, and actions. The thing about the culture being the air or the water is that some of us, namely those of who are BIPOC, can very clearly identify white supremacy in the air and water and can point to how white supremacy is reflected in cultural norms, values, beliefs, standards, those who hold value, and narratives. As a Black person, I understand white supremacy is constantly in play because my whole being is deeply affected by white supremacy in every way.

White-bodied people are not socialized to understand how white supremacy infuses the air and water. Cultural norms created by white-bodied people are designed to benefit white people and to uphold the system of white supremacy. These cultural norms perpetuate the notion that white people are the norm and normal. White-bodied people can move through their entire lives without identifying the fact they live in a white supremacy culture and benefit from it. They don't have to see the air or the water because they aren't aware they are in it. Meanwhile, white supremacy is constantly reminding BIPOC people that we are not white and therefore not normal.

Cultural norms connected to systems of power such as white supremacy, capitalism, heterosexism, sexism, ableism, and all systems designed to oppress entire groups of people who are less proximal to power are influential in shaping how we think of ourselves and how we perceive others. Cultural norms shape how we experience the world and navigate our lives. Some of the cultural norms and narratives perpetuated by white supremacy culture about BIPOC people that BIPOC people have internalized and need to heal from include these:

Black people are criminals.

Black people are untrustworthy.

Black people do not take care of their communities.

Indigenous people are savages.

Indigenous people are extinct or their cultures are dead.

Latinx people are loud.

Latinx males have machismo.

Latinx people are undocumented.

People of Asian descent are the model minority.

People of Asian descent are all from China and brought the terrible "China virus," otherwise known as COVID-19, to America.

I have not named every ethnicity or race in this list of messages. If you embody an ethnicity or racial identity that is not listed above, please take some time to consider the race-based messages you have received about yourself and the messages you have learned about other People of Color from the culture of white supremacy. These narratives are deeply damaging, and so often BIPOC affinity group facilitators and space-holders are responding to what manifests for us from internalizing negative messages about what it means to be Black, Indigenous, or a Person of Color. We will explore this more deeply when we delve into internalized racial oppression in chapter 3.

The organization dRworks defines cultural racism as the way in which the dominant culture is

> founded upon and then defines and shapes norms, values, beliefs and standards to advantage white people and oppress BIPOC communities and people. The ways in which the dominant culture defines reality to advantage white people and oppress BIPOC communities and people. The norms, values, or standards assumed by the dominant society that perpetuate racism. Examples: thin, blond, white women as the basis for our society's standard of beauty; women on welfare assumed to be Black or Brown and portrayed as irresponsible while white-collar fraud in the business community is costing the US hundreds of billions of dollars a year; requiring people to speak English historically (Indigenous peoples) and today (people from Central and South America) as a way of deliberately destroying community and culture.[6]

The level not represented in the preceding analyses is interpersonal racism. For purposes of the analysis I offered and for your own understanding, you might use personal and interpersonal synonymously.

Interpersonal and personal racism is what I was socialized to believe was the definition of all types of racism, including institutional and cultural. Interpersonal racism is when a white-bodied person expresses racial bias towards a BIPOC person. It is often this type of racism that is highlighted when a famous white-bodied person does something that is racist, like use a racial epithet. Often they are pointed out as an individual who did something racist, ignoring that they live in a culture that has socialized them to be racist. In my mind, there is no way to separate personal and interpersonal from institutional and cultural racism.

THE FOUR FOUNDATIONS OF RACISM

Finally, to understand very clearly why we would need affinity groups we need to understand the Four Foundations of Racism (see figure 1.2).[7]

The Four Foundations represent how racism, internalized white supremacy, and internalized racial inferiority manifest from the system of white supremacy. Racism and internalized white superiority manifest from an ideology and belief system that white is superior, hence white supremacy. Because there is racism, BIPOC people are internalizing messages that being BIPOC is inferior, therefore internalizing racial inferiority. In part, the Four Foundations are in play whenever we meet in affinity groups by race to process what we have internalized from white supremacy culture about our racial identity.

This chapter provided an overview of shared language and an analysis of power specific to white supremacy and racism to level-set. It is

FIGURE 1.2

White Supremacy	Racism
Internalized White Supremacy	Internalized Racial Inferiority

important for you, as a facilitator of a BIPOC affinity group, to have language to reach people and an analysis of personal, institutional, and cultural racism. Shared language and the analysis can help you better understand yourself as a BIPOC person, understand the reasons why someone is behaving as they are in an affinity group, equip you with tools like language and understanding, and support you if you are leading affinity groups within institutions and communities. As clarified before, my own experience of learning language and the power of analysis was liberating for me and gave me a much deeper understanding of what had been happening to me all my life as I navigated a white supremacy culture. In the next chapter I will share more about why we meet in affinity groups and the importance of these groups as a tool for reducing harm and promoting healing for BIPOC people.

"Our only chance at dismantling racial injustice is being more curious about its origins than we are worried about our comfort. It's not a comfortable conversation for any of us. It is risky and messy. It is haunting work to recall the sins of our past. But is this not the work we have been called to anyway? Is this not the work of the Holy Spirit to illuminate truth and inspire transformation? It's haunting. But it's also holy."

—AUSTIN CHANNING, *I'm Still Here: Black Dignity in a World Made for Whiteness*

CHAPTER 2

A PLACE WHERE WE CAN BE

*People of color need their own spaces. . . . We need places in which we can
gather and be free from the mainstream stereotypes and marginalization
that permeate every other societal space we occupy. We need spaces
where we can be our authentic selves without white people's judgment
and insecurity muzzling that expression. We need spaces where we can
simply be—where we can get off the treadmill of making white people
comfortable and finally realize just how tired we are.*

—KELSEY BLACKWELL, *The Arrow*, 2018

THIS CHAPTER DEFINES what affinity groups are and explains why we meet
in affinity groups and how they can serve as a harm reduction strategy
in the work of dismantling racism. In chapters 5, 6, and 7, I offer information about what to consider if one wants to facilitate, how to facilitate,
some thoughts on what content to offer in a BIPOC affinity space, and
some practices I have found to be useful over my two decades of leading
BIPOC affinity spaces.

WHAT ARE AFFINITY GROUPS?

Affinity groups are formed when a group of people who share a similar
identity come together to process feelings, connect, build community,
strategize, and heal. This identity can be based on race; gender identity;
sexual orientation; social class; mental, physical, and emotional ability or
disability; or other identities or experiences. Racial affinity groups are
groups that form on the basis of a racial identity—white or BIPOC, or
sometimes Black. Indigenous, and other People of Color are split into
different affinity groups on the basis of ethnicity or race. It is common in

racial equity work to use affinity spaces as a tool for further learning and development, and so white-bodied and BIPOC people can share thoughts and process feelings about white supremacy and racism in separate spaces and explore what these systems are doing to them because of their embodied racial identity.

Prior to my first dismantling racism training, I had not met in a formal affinity group. I had been in all-Black or BIPOC spaces before—like church, family gatherings, some community events, and the ballet class my mother sent me to at the community center when I was a young child or with family. BIPOC have a long history of creating our own spaces out of necessity because of our experience of being othered and our desire to create safer spaces for ourselves. The spaces just mentioned were designed to be Black- or BIPOC-only spaces because of white supremacy, but there was never an explicit naming that our purpose in coming together was a strategy to respond to white supremacy, racism, and internalized racial oppression.

I experienced my first BIPOC affinity group when I attended my first dismantling racism training when I was twenty-three. Right before the facilitators of the training shared that we would be breaking into affinity groups, they said that we would be talking about racial identity development and internalized racial oppression in the BIPOC affinity group and internalized white superiority in the white affinity group. At that point in my life, my understanding of my racial identity had been informed by my lived experience as a Black person, messages I received from my family and community, my experience interacting with and moving through institutions, and the white cultural norms I observed being uplifted by dominant culture.

Growing up I knew I was Black, and from a young age I observed how Black people were treated differently than white-bodied people. I heard my mother talking about her experience as a special education teacher working in inner-city Richmond and how the educational system didn't take care of Black children. This mirrored the experience I was having in a predominantly white school. I experienced a system that didn't take care of me or other students of color. I was the only Black girl in my class until fifth grade. I remember it being a big deal when Folayan, a young Black girl like me, decided to come to my school. Finally, there were two of us. As I moved through middle and high school, I heard assumptions being made about my capacity, potential, and skill level. For some reason, in senior year it shocked all of my teachers—except for two—when they discovered I had gotten into every one of the colleges I had applied to. This happened on the heels of a guidance counselor saying she wouldn't help me with my applications; she told me I wouldn't get into college.

In church I heard my minister speak of the resilience we as Black people embodied in spite of living in a white supremacy culture. Every Sunday after church I sat around my grandmother's table and heard stories about how white supremacy worked to keep us in our place—marginalized and disempowered. I also heard stories about Black pride and how we as BIPOC have thrived even as the system of white supremacy has worked to disrupt and dismantle the conditions we have put in place to find freedom. Neither the minister in church nor my grandmother used the term "white supremacy" when they talked about our embodied resilience or about experiences of marginalization, but they were certainly naming what they understood about power and they were telling me how the white supremacy culture operated.

I learned about Blackness and Black culture on television as well. I grew up watching *Good Times* and *The Jeffersons* on our little TV in the kitchen while my mother cooked dinner every weekday evening. These shows were vastly different from one another, but the struggle many Black people experience as a result of white supremacy was a theme in both. The Jeffersons worked to move on up and the Evans family in *Good Times* worked to make ends meet, never having enough to move up to the tower in the sky. My mother would always watch the six o'clock and eleven o'clock news. When I watched with her, I learned how Black people and other BIPOC are portrayed as criminals just for being who they are in the world. With the exception of the times I spent with my family and church community, the current that ran through all of the other places I frequented, in which I learned about my Black identity, was that Blackness wasn't valued and was instead underestimated.

As we sat in the dismantling racism training, waiting to break up into our affinity groups, I felt a nervousness in my body and the room. It was confusing to some that we would separate in a training that was ultimately designed for us to raise our consciousness and take collective action together across lines of difference. The facilitators explained that each group had different things to process related to racial identity. Even though their explanation was valid, it didn't ease some of the nervousness and anxiety I sensed in the space as each group prepared to go to their respective meetings.

While I understood that BIPOC and white-bodied people lived a different experience in the world based on race, the nervousness I felt while preparing to separate from the group as a whole was based on a curiosity about how we, as a collective, could heal from the trauma of white supremacy—the ways it has lied to and harmed us all—by separating into two groups. I knew the trauma that white-bodied and BIPOC people experienced wasn't the same; I knew that it didn't live in the body in the same way; but I didn't yet understand that we needed two different spaces to name, work through, and heal our trauma.

Nervousness also emerged from remembering the numerous occasions when I had not been accepted by—and was, at times, ostracized by—other Black people because they believed I wasn't "Black enough." Even though I was used to moving in spaces where Black and white folks didn't fully accept me, it stung worse when Black people didn't accept me for who I was. I believed other Black people should have known and felt our shared struggle and interconnectedness. We had all experienced systemic racism and were struggling against a system that wanted to control our bodies, annihilate us, and deny us access to freedom.

As we broke into our affinity spaces, I was aware of the value of learning more about identity, internalizations, and empowerment. Still, initially, I didn't understand how much the affinity space would deepen my perception and understanding of myself. I didn't understand how much I would come to learn why other Black people might not have accepted me in the past. The affinity group explained so much to me about my development as a Black person and how the white supremacy culture affected me and communities of color. The affinity group grew my understanding of the systems I had been born into and inherited, messages I received about myself and race, and the power of cultural conditioning.

LADDER OF EMPOWERMENT FOR PEOPLE OF COLOR

The lens in which racial identity was talked about in our affinity space was through a ladder of empowerment developed by Kenneth Jones, who, after the first dismantling racism training I attended, became my colleague in a training collective for many years in what was to become Dismantling Racism Works (it was then called Changeworks). Kenneth was a vibrant soul who dedicated his life to dismantling white supremacy, creating conditions for liberation for all, and especially for his BIPOC brothers, sisters, and comrades. He was also committed to bringing fun and humor into his work. I remember the first time I met him to learn more about Changeworks as I considered becoming a trainer with their collective. Kenneth's smile was contagious. His laugh was deep bellied, and in my experience, he was unapologetically himself. Kenneth was an organizer, leader, visionary, colleague, and friend.

The ladder of empowerment has eight rungs, or stages (see figure 2.1). My perception is that Kenneth was able to write and speak of the stages so eloquently because of his lived experience as a Black man and as someone deeply committed to collective liberation. The ladder feels representative of Kenneth's vision for us as People of Color and for the collective to take collective action, build a community of resistance, and to understand to our core how collective care is a strategy toward creating racial equity and dismantling racial injustice. Kenneth passed away in 2004. I believe that he, like other souls who work so tirelessly trying to combat white supremacy, experienced dis-ease in his body as a result of his efforts. My hope for Kenneth is that he experiences much ease in the afterlife and that his legacy lives on in communities, organizing circles, collectives, and this world.

FIGURE 2.1

THE LADDER OF EMPOWERMENT

Community of Resistance

Collective Action

Challenging

Investigation

Self-Awareness

Exclusion/Immersion

Rage/Depression

Not White

LEARNING YOU ARE NOT WHITE The first stage or rung of the ladder represents our experience when we as BIPOC people learn we are not white. This can happen through an encounter with a white person or with an institution that has been designed to serve white-bodied people and oppress BIPOC people. Often this happens at a young age, and it can send us into crisis. Once we realize we aren't white, often our first reaction is to try to become white. This can happen through the way we dress or wear our hair, or by speaking in a way that emulates white culture. Another response to learning we aren't white is trying to be "as good as whites." At this stage we view whiteness as the model of humanity. We might try to become this model of humanity as a plea to be treated humanely. We may want what white people have and strive to get it at any cost. This stage can bring about depression and sometimes suicidality because we are constantly being reminded by the dominant culture that we aren't white. This rung of the ladder can result in our becoming angry because we cannot change who we are or how dominant culture views us.

RAGE AND DEPRESSION This anger can lead to rage, the next rung on the Ladder of Empowerment for People of Color. Rage is the stage where we become angry at white-bodied people. We become angry at the situation we are living in (a racist and white supremacy culture), angry about how we have been treated historically and how we continue to be treated unfairly and inhumanely. We become angry about the oppression we as BIPOC people have experienced. Sometimes rage can lead to our attacking white people in a variety of ways. In my work as a racial equity educator in many racially mixed settings, I am often in spaces where BIPOC people have no patience with or compassion for white-bodied people. Sometimes in these spaces, white-bodied people are shut down before they open their mouths to speak, share, or ask a question. Sometimes, this replicates behaviors that are not based on abolition but instead oppression. I understand these reactions and behaviors, and I question whether they leave us feeling more empowered. Perhaps we might temporarily feel satisfied or pleasured by expressing our rage in a way that causes more trauma and pain to others, but in my experience, this sense of satisfaction is fleeting and doesn't leave me feeling empowered. This is because, while I am rageful about white supremacy, and my rage might move me into action, it can also consume me. Empowerment for me in this stage would be to recognize my rage, understand how I want to express it and what it is doing to me, and transmute it into something that will heal myself and the collective.

EXCLUSION AND IMMERSION In the next stage of empowerment, exclusion and immersion, we purposefully exclude white people from our lives in order to immerse ourselves in our culture. We find ourselves spending time only with other BIPOC people and learning as much as we can about our racial identity and ethnicity. Some of us remain in this stage for a while. Exclusion and immersion can be healing, especially if we haven't had the opportunity to be in BIPOC-only spaces or spaces representative of our specific racial identity or ethnicity.

SELF-AWARENESS Self-awareness follows our time of exclusion and immersion. In this stage we become more aware of our cultural history and ourselves. This is the work we do to better understand our place and positionality in history and the world.

INVESTIGATION Investigation is the next rung on the ladder. This is a time where we not only continue to become aware of our history, positionality, and place in the world but also study the culture and history of white-bodied people. Given that our histories are intertwined, once we have studied more about the racial hierarchy and how "white" became a term used to separate us and justify systems like slavery, capitalism, and patriarchy, we have a better understanding of ourselves.

CHALLENGING The next stage is where we begin to challenge white-bodied people with our knowledge and what we have learned in the previous stages. Many of us are conditioned to believe we cannot and should not oppose white-bodied people. During this stage we learn how to challenge white-bodied people effectively. For me, this means challenging white-bodied people with the true history of how we came to be living in the way we are in this particular moment. It means not allowing white people to steal my joy or happiness. It means not expending all of my energy trying to convince white-bodied people that racism and white supremacy are real. To me, this stage has meant focusing on how I want to use my energy and on the question of how to challenge without exhausting myself in the process.

COLLECTIVE ACTION The next stage is collective action, which happens when we feel ready to build and work together across lines of difference. In this stage, we recognize that our liberation is bound up with that of white people and that both BIPOC and white-bodied people have a role in interrupting, disrupting, and dismantling white supremacy and racism.

COMMUNITY OF RESISTANCE Collective action leads to the final stage of empowerment—the stage of building a community of resistance. When we are part of a community of resistance, we organize together for collective power and work to create conditions for everyone to thrive. We center healing in our work and strive to heal from racism and what we have internalized about ourselves because we live in a white supremacy culture. A community of resistance continues to develop as we hone critical thinking skills and deepen our understanding of community, the country, and the world. A community of resistance develops leadership and a system of accountability, which speaks to how we come into community together and what we will do when harm happens in our community of resistance.

As each of these stages was explained to me, I felt a resonance with the other BIPOC people in the room. I reviewed my life up until that point and remembered an encounter, which may not have been my first but is the first one I can remember, when I realized I wasn't white. A white child on the playground called me a "nigger." I had never heard the word before and went home to ask my mother about it. She promptly pulled out a massive Webster's dictionary, which still had the word "nigger" in it, and she read the definition. She proceeded to have a talk with me about how I was not a nigger, and then went on making dinner for us. As she explained the etymology of the word, it felt like she was having a conversation about what was on the menu for dinner. There was something ominously rote about the way she explained the origin of the word. I imagine she had been called the n-word many times and was likely waiting for the moment when I would come home and ask her what it meant. What feels interesting about this experience is that when this happened on the playground, my best friend at the time, Alison, who was white, yelled at the white child. For years and to this day, I am curious about what made Alison stand up for me. I wonder what she had internalized about herself or what she understood about the world that made her disrupt the child's behavior instead of corroborating the white child's assumption that I was a nigger.

I remember experiencing the stage of exclusion and immersion. When I was in college I joined the Black Student Movement (BSM). I wanted to learn more about "the movement" and to be in space with other Black students. Even though my joining the BSM was a way to immerse myself in my culture, their meetings and ethos left me feeling more excluded. It was as if I had to prove that I was part of the Black group by pulling out my "Black girl" card.

I remember the stage of collective action. From a young age I understood that the world treated people differently depending on the identities they embodied. I knew oppression existed before I had the words to describe how it felt to be oppressed. I felt disconnected and witnessed disconnection, especially across lines of difference. These things, coupled with attending a predominantly white school, made me curious about how to relate across lines of difference. Working toward collective action and in a community of resistance never felt foreign to me. Collective action, community, and building a movement of resistance are aligned with my values and very being. That first experience in the POC affinity group did change my perspective about myself, others, and the world. It opened a pathway for me to do the work I had always been curious about—working across lines of difference to create conditions for our collective healing.

Something to note about these stages of empowerment is that in real life they are not linear in the way the ladder presents them. We move up and down the ladder, and in large part this depends on what is happening in our lives and the world. For example, every time I hear about another Black or Brown person being killed by a police officer, I become enraged. I feel rage for every loss we have experienced as BIPOC people. Feeling rage makes it difficult for me to be in community with white-bodied people and to organize together in a community of resistance. When I am in a meeting and made to feel invisible and the experience feels racialized, I remember that I am not white. Consciously I know I am not white, but dominant culture works to continue to remind me of this fact and the reality that I will be treated differently because I am not white. The ladder is a guide for us to better understand our experience as BIPOC people, and I encourage you to remember that we are not fixed in time. We are evolving all of the time; as conditions shift in our lives and the world, we do, too.

As a person who is interested in holding space for yourself and other BIPOC people, take a moment to consider the different stages of empowerment and experiences you have had at each stage.

- Do you remember the experience of learning you weren't white?
- Do you know how it felt to learn this in a world that values whiteness over being a Person of Color?
- Have you felt rage or anger for yourself and your ancestors?
- If you moved through a stage of exclusion and immersion, what did you learn from fully immersing yourself in your culture? How did it feel to deepen your self-awareness of yourself and community?
- Do you have a dream of moving into collective action with others to dismantle racism?
- Do you envision working with others to together create a community of resistance?

In addition to going through the stages of the ladder of empowerment, we meet in affinity groups to share how we experience internalized racial inferiority and what manifests from it. I will explore this more and offer a framework in chapter 3. BIPOC people meet in affinity groups to build relationships and community with other BIPOC people who are deeply affected by white supremacy. We meet in affinity groups to learn more about how white supremacy thrives when we, as BIPOC people, are unable to see the commonality in the experiences we have when navigating a white supremacy culture. We meet in affinity groups to heal our hearts, spirits, and bodies and to decolonize our minds. We meet in affinity groups to create conditions where harm is less likely to occur from the ways whiteness operates.

While we sat in our POC affinity space in that first dismantling racism training I attended, the white-bodied people were in their own affinity space. They discussed the Ladder of Racial Identity Development—a multistep program analogous to the Ladder of Empowerment for People of Color.[1] They discussed issues such as denial and defensiveness, guilt and shame, acknowledging and opening up, taking responsibility and self-righteousness, collective action, and a community of resistance. The content in a white affinity space and a BIPOC affinity space ultimately lead us to a similar place—a community of resistance. How we get to a place of resistance is different for white-bodied people, given that white supremacy is unrelenting and ever-present in our lives as BIPOC people.

HARM REDUCTION

The work of creating racial justice isn't easy, and as we work together in racially mixed spaces to create this kind of justice, harm will happen. One of the assumptions listed in chapter 1 is: There is no way to talk about racism without the risk of replicating it. This assumption speaks to the reality that white-bodied people and BIPOC people have different experiences as we navigate a white supremacy culture. This assumption also speaks to the fact that we as BIPOC people are living in a white supremacy culture, and almost every part of our lives—if not all of them—are in some way affected by white supremacy.

White-bodied people are living in a white supremacy culture as well, and to varying degrees—due to other identities that intersect with their racial identity of white—benefit psychically, economically, physically, emotionally, and spiritually from white supremacy. When we come together with white-bodied people in a shared space focused on dismantling racism, often racism is replicated because white-bodied people are learning about white supremacy and internalized white superiority, and often this learning takes place at the expense of us as BIPOC people.

We understand how racism and white supremacy operate, and white-bodied people have to learn about it to better understand it; still, even with continued learning and study, white-bodied people will not fully understand what it is to be BIPOC people in a white supremacy culture. While white-bodied people are learning, we continue to perish because of white supremacy. In general, often there is a tension in racially mixed spaces, and this tension can intensify quite a bit when there is a focus on racial equity. White-bodied people's limitations around fully understanding our experience as being BIPOC and the exhaustion we feel because of having to try to survive in a white supremacy culture, coupled with the reality that white-bodied people cannot learn and change fast enough, can feel like being stuck in a maze with no clear pathway out. The dynamic in which white-bodied people inherently experience a lack of understanding of our experience as BIPOC people, and the dynamic of learning about versus living the ways in which white supremacy tries to invalidate our very existence, is what I call the *lived-learned dynamic*. As BIPOC people, we are living racism—racism is happening to us—whereas white-bodied people are learning about it. A lived experience of a form of oppression is very different from learning about it. This is one reason why affinity groups are so necessary to our work in dismantling racism. Affinity groups give us a moment to be in a space with each other, knowing there is some level of shared understanding about our lived experience. For this reason, affinity groups can serve as a harm reduction strategy as we work toward the goal of dismantling racism.

The older I get, the less I trust white people. So having spaces where I feel protected is essential. Even in the chaos and messiness that can arise in affinity spaces, they are vital to my very existence.

—JEANINE ABRAHAM

We do not live in a harm-free world. We live in a world where acts of violence and harm routinely occur. Harm is inflicted *upon those* with less power, and we do not yet have clear systems of accountability that do not replicate systems of oppression. Given this context, and that we as a collective have not yet completely dismantled racism and white supremacy, harm will happen as we come together to do the work of learning what we need to do and practice as we dismantle racism and white supremacy. (In chapter 7, I discuss specifically how harm can emerge in our affinity spaces as a result of intersections of different identities.)

As defined in the "Shared Language" section of chapter 1, harm is connected to systems of oppression and the ways people within systems and culture create conditions for us to be less or more proximal to power based on the identities we embody—in this case, white-bodied people, institutions led and controlled by white-bodied people, and white-bodied people who implicitly and explicitly perpetuate cultural norms that uphold the notion that white is superior. In racially mixed spaces, harm can happen because of the lived learned dynamic mentioned above and because white-bodied people and BIPOC people can be in different stages of racial identity development and empowerment. These stages can collide and make a seemingly safer space for learning very unsafe for BIPOC people within seconds.

We meet in affinity spaces to heal all the fractures and wounds white supremacy has inflicted on us. We meet in affinity spaces because we need a space to process our experience as BIPOC people without white-bodied people expressing defensiveness and denying our experience of systemic racism and oppression. We need a space to process without white-bodied folks congratulating themselves on recognizing their whiteness and realizing their whiteness is a weapon they inherited at birth because they were born into a white supremacy culture that benefits them and oppresses us. We need a space where we do not have to watch white-bodied people do what they so often do in anti-racism spaces—compete for the title of who is the "most woke" in the space. White-bodied people need a space where they can develop the skill of calling each other out, in, and up, so we do not always have to be the ones who do this labor.

White-bodied people need a space where they can process without our caretaking them, a behavioral pattern that is deeply ingrained in us. This pattern is ancestral because our ancestors and we have had to maintain white comfort to stay safe and alive. We need a reprieve from whiteness. We need a space of our own, one in which we can be with each other and experience less harm than we do as we navigate a world that prioritizes the needs of white-bodied people, teaches us we are less than because we are BIPOC people, and demands that we assuage the discomfort and fragility white-bodied people face as they participate in the transformative work and practice of dismantling racism.

In my years of facilitating, my understanding of how meeting in BIPOC affinity spaces can mitigate harm has grown. Each time I have either called for an affinity space myself or witnessed someone do that in a space I am facilitating or participating in, there has been a clear intention, and often it has been to create a safer space for oneself. The separation is purposeful and intentional. It is so we can have room to exhale with each other. It is so we can have room to see and witness each other. It is so we can call in our ancestors and remember who we are because of who they were to us. I have seen BIPOC people call for an affinity space when they are tired of harm being inflicted upon them. I have seen BIPOC people call for an affinity space when an issue needed to be addressed, and some strategy needed to be developed in order to address it. BIPOC people have called to meet in an affinity space to create a list of demands for the white-bodied people in the room.

Meeting in the affinity group during my first dismantling racism training felt like a breath of fresh air and, at the same time, a deep exhale. I felt more expansive, as if I could exhale more deeply because I was in space with people who understood something about my experience of being Black in a world we are still loudly calling on to value Blackness. The first affinity space I was part of and almost every affinity space since that time has felt like a healing salve. Affinity spaces are indeed medicine for my heart and spirit. I believe the work of dismantling racism at its core is about bringing us back into wholeness. Bringing us back into our humanity. Healing ourselves so we do not harm others. Affinity spaces are a way to explore how our unattended hurt can lead to hurting others, how the system of white supremacy is set up to divide us from ourselves and each other. Affinity spaces are a powerful and profound way to reclaim our wholeness and humanity.

Here I provide some journaling prompts for you to contemplate why race-based affinity groups are a harm reduction strategy.

- How do you feel about engaging the tool of meeting in racial affinity groups in your racial equity work? In your experience, why are they an important tool?
- How might you explain the need for us to separate to do our work to dismantle racism as BIPOC people?
- If you have had the experience of being in a BIPOC affinity space, how have you seen the tool of meeting in affinity groups based on race mitigate harm?
- If you have not had the experience of attending or facilitating a BIPOC affinity space, how do you imagine race-based affinity spaces could reduce harm in racially mixed spaces where people are working across lines of difference?
- In your experience or imagination, how can affinity groups lead to deeper healing for us as BIPOC people?

"It is in our collectivities we find reservoirs of hope and optimism."

—ANGELA DAVIS, *Freedom Is a Constant Struggle: Ferguson, Palestine, and the Foundations of a Movement*

CHAPTER 3

EVERY CHILD'S TREASURE

*Adults, older girls, shops, magazines, newspapers, window signs—
all the world had agreed that a blue-eyed, yellow-haired,
pink-skinned doll was every girl child's treasure.*

—TONI MORRISON, *The Bluest Eye*

D URING MY SENIOR YEAR of high school I went to the doctor, who, after
weighing me, promptly told me I was obese. I was seventeen years
old, weighed 170 pounds, was five feet five and a half inches, and played
sports almost all year long. My legs were strong enough for me to play
sweeper in soccer and field hockey. I had broad shoulders like my father,
and my arms were very strong. I knew I was sturdy—not stocky, but sturdy.
Upon hearing the news from my doctor that I was overweight, I decided
to go on a diet. Instead of continuing to eat the pizza that the people
working in the cafeteria used to put in the microwave and then hand to
us through the little window via which we got our food, or the subs from
Stuffy's Subs in Richmond, I made salads with low-fat dressing and had
fruit for lunch. I ate as few carbs as I could and continued to play sports,
but instead of playing them for fun, I now played them to lose weight. I
lost twenty pounds my senior year of high school and headed to college
weighing 150 pounds.

In college, during first-year orientation, I remember going to the dining hall with my mother and grandmother. It had a huge salad bar, a stir-
fry station, pizza, fries, chicken wings, and more. It felt like the Taj Mahal
of dining. Even though there were plenty of foods to select from, I decided to continue my diet and frequent the salad bar for most of my meals
during my first year of college. I also decided to work out for at least an
hour each day. I would ride the exercise bike in the gym and then take a

step class and walk back to my dorm. As I embarked on a path of living a "healthier lifestyle" by losing weight through dieting and exercising, I lost my way. Things got out of control. I went from frequenting the salad bar and exercising an hour a day to existing off of SweeTARTS and coffee, exercising as much as I could, and not sleeping.

I had an eating disorder. According to the *Diagnostic and Statistical Manual of Mental Disorders*, my specific diagnosis was "eating disorder; unspecified." My disordered eating and obsession with exercise meant I didn't meet the diagnostic criteria for anorexia or bulimia. I tried throwing up after meals, but that didn't work, so I became addicted to laxatives. I had severe insomnia because my body was malnourished and waiting for when the next meal, if any, would come.

I was attending a predominantly white college after attending predominantly white schools from first grade through my senior year. The standard of beauty presented to me by my white peers and the media was a thin, white, blonde, heterosexual, abled, cisgender woman. The system of capitalism doubled down on the standard of beauty by convincing me I needed to buy things to alter my body and make it thin, sexy, and desirable. I am convinced my eating disorder manifested from my own sense of worthlessness because of what white supremacy, the patriarchy, and capitalism—three deeply interwoven systems—had taught me about myself as a woman and a Black person.

As I was growing up, my body size and shape weren't the only things I wanted to change. From the age of fourteen up until now, I have had my hair relaxed. This means that every six to eight weeks I have chemicals put in my hair to straighten it and to tame its natural texture. To be fair to myself, I have never been very good at doing my own hair, so in large part I get a relaxer put in my hair to make it more manageable for me to work with. Even so, I cannot help but believe that the standard of beauty presented to us by our white supremacy culture convinced my great-grandmother, Angie, my grandmothers Sally and Dorothy, my mother, Clara, and me to straighten our hair because to have "nappy," or natural, hair would not be beautiful or proper.

In addition to straightening my hair and developing an eating disorder that took years to heal from and is still an issue at times, I have had three significant romantic relationships with Black men. All the rest, including a seventeen-year relationship, have been with white men. I am not judging my choice to date white men, because I do believe we love whom we love, but I have been socialized into a white supremacy culture—a culture that at every turn has told me and us that being Black and a person of color isn't worthy, valid, or tasteful. A culture that at every turn has told me and us that white is better and superior to being a "Body of Culture."

INTERNALIZED RACIAL OPPRESSION

My eating disorder, straightened hair, and attraction to white-bodied men all emerged from what I have internalized about Blackness from white supremacy culture. Internalized racial oppression or internalized racial inferiority refers to the internalization by BIPOC people of the images, stereotypes, prejudices, and myths promoted by the racist system about BIPOC people. Our thoughts and feelings about ourselves, people of our own racial group, or other BIPOC people are based on the racist messages we receive from the broader system. Dominant white supremacy culture perpetuates the message that BIPOC people are inferior in many ways—messages such as "Black people are lazy," "Latinx people are illegal," "Black people are criminals and a threat," and "Asians are the model minority." These messages and many more are internalized by us, and certain behaviors manifest: self-doubt, self-hate, addiction, colorism, violence, anxiety, depression, powerlessness, apathy, self-destruction, division, and becoming withdrawn. These behaviors work to break down our bodies, minds, and spirits.

> "The very serious function of racism is a distraction. It keeps you from doing your work. It keeps you explaining over and over again, your reason for being."
> —TONI MORRISON, speech at Portland State University, 1975

As you lead BIPOC affinity spaces, it is important to understand internalized racial oppression, to be able to explain and define internalized racial oppression, to offer a framework to better understand how it affects us, to share examples of what you have internalized with the affinity group, and to engage in a continuous process of self-awareness around how internalized racial oppression continues to affect you. In the next section I offer a framework that I routinely use when leading BIPOC affinity spaces and I will ask you to reflect on different parts of the framework in preparation for leading a BIPOC affinity group.

THE SELF-SYSTEM

This framework was shared with me by my friend and colleague Vivette Jeffries-Logan. Vivette attended a conference where Raúl Quiñones-Rosado, a liberation psychologist, author, and racial justice educator-organizer, presented a framework that was set up similarly to a medicine wheel. For a long time, our training collective, of which Vivette was a part, had been using the Ladder of Empowerment for People of Color (see chapter 2). The Ladder is a powerful tool, but we needed something else to complement it that would clearly explain how we are affected by and might heal from internalized racial oppression. After Vivette saw Raúl's framework, she came back to our training collective excited to share a new model with us called the self-system. Something I deeply appreciate about the self-system is its holistic view of the self. This framework sees us as more than a body and takes into account our thoughts, emotions, and spirit. It has the capacity to allow us to explore and heal the whole of who we are. The self-system (see figure 3.1) is a way to illustrate how white supremacy affects us as individual BIPOC people, the community of color(s) we come from, and other communities of color.

FIGURE 3.1

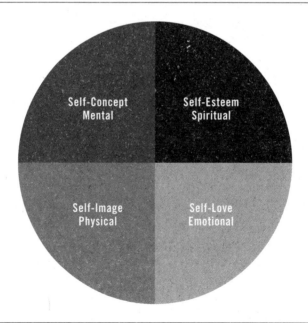

The self-system is composed of four parts: physical, mental, emotional, and spiritual. Each one of these parts is associated with our perception of self, which is influenced by the information and messages we take in about ourselves from the dominant culture. The physical is associated with self-image; the mental, with self-concept; the emotional, with self-love; and the spiritual, with self-esteem. We constantly take in information from various people, institutions, systems, and cultural norms created by white supremacy culture about who we are on the basis of our constructed racialized identities. The self-system invites us to consider what messages we are taking in and how they affect us physically, emotionally, spiritually, and mentally. The self-system may not represent how you would describe yourself. I will ask you to reflect on it and invite you to feel free to use different words to describe how you think of yourself and the parts of who you are (see figure 3.2).

FIGURE 3.2

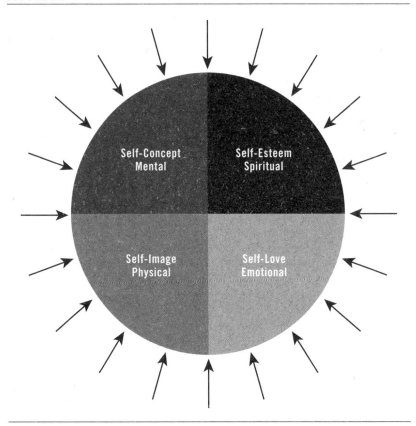

For example, white supremacy culture has communicated to me that Black people are dangerous, criminals, and untrustworthy. White supremacy culture has perpetuated a message that Black people are working the system and taking advantage of welfare and social services. In 2011, Newt Gingrich kicked off his campaign for the Republican Party's presidential nomination by deriding Barack Obama as "the most successful food stamp president in American history."[1] This statement harked back to the Reagan administration's rhetoric about deadbeat dads, most often portrayed as a stereotypical Black man who wasn't taking care of his children and a welfare queen most often portrayed as a bigger-bodied Black woman with a shopping cart and children falling out of it while using her food stamps to pay for soft drinks. A message that we do not take care of ourselves or each other is perpetuated by white supremacy, and the additional underlying message is that we do not know how to take care of ourselves. Black people are told we are lazy, ugly, and worthless.

The white supremacy culture has perpetuated messages about other BIPOC people. One such message is that Latinx people are illegal in the United States, as if they had created their own borders and the US hadn't stolen their land overnight. In fact, from 1846 to 1848, in the Mexican-American War, the US invaded Mexico for its land and resources. The war ended with the Treaty of Guadalupe Hidalgo, which transferred over 55 percent of Mexican territory to the US, land that became all or part of ten states: Arizona, California, New Mexico, Texas, Oklahoma, Kansas, Wyoming, Colorado, Nevada, and Utah. The treaty promised to protect the lands, language, and culture of the Mexicans who were living in the ceded territory, but Congress substituted a "Protocol" that required Mexicans to prove in court that they had "legitimate" title to their lands. Unable to provide proof in a culture that did not record land transactions, the "Protocol" became the legal basis for the massive theft of land from Mexicans in these territories.

Messages are perpetuated that Indigenous people are savage, extinct, or belong to a dead culture. These messages connect back to the time in our history when Indigenous people were taken to boarding schools, away from their Native lands and families, were given haircuts and English names, and were forbidden to speak their Native languages. The motto of many of these schools was "Kill the Indian, Save the Child" because Native Americans, people indigenous to the land we now call the United States of America, were seen as subhuman and savage by white-bodied individuals, institutions controlled by white-bodied people, and the cultural norms perpetuated by a white supremacy culture. The white supremacy culture maintained a message that Native Americans' souls needed to be saved and elevated to white standards through a process of forced assimilation.

The white supremacy culture has created negative narratives about people of Asian descent, most recently in response to COVID-19. Prior to COVID-19, people of Asian descent were strategically framed as the "model minority" to pit them against other People of Color who were lower in the racial hierarchy, which placed white at the top, Black at the bottom, and other People of Color between the two bookends of the hierarchy, white and Black (see chapter 4 for more discussion of the racial hierarchy). Sarah-Soonling Blackburn, an educator, speaker, and professional learning facilitator, describes the myth of the model minority in the following way:

> The myth of the model minority is based on stereotypes. It perpetuates a narrative in which Asian American children are whiz kids or musical geniuses. Within the myth of the model minority, Tiger Moms (a strict or demanding mother who demands their child reaches high levels of achievement) force children to work harder and be better than everyone else. . . . This myth characterizes Asian Americans as a polite, law-abiding group who have achieved a higher level of success than the general population through some combination of innate talent and pull-yourselves-up-by-your-bootstraps immigrant striving.[2]

The white supremacy culture fabricates narratives about every community of color as a strategy to uphold the idea that white is superior and being a person of color is inferior.

In the rest of this chapter, I ask you to reflect on several journaling prompts to surface negative internalized messages. The questions and activities in these prompts may not be easy for you to reflect on, and they may trigger your nervous system. I will ask you to think about the negative messages you have internalized about yourself on the basis of your race. Before diving into the journaling prompts, you might choose to take some deep breaths, prepare a cup of tea, or engage in any activity that might support your nervous system and help you feel more grounded and stable as you reflect on the questions and prompts. Take your time to move through them and take breaks as necessary.

THE MESSAGES I HAVE INTERNALIZED

Take a moment to consider the negative messages you have taken in from the dominant culture about your racial identity. This is not an invitation to consider the positive messages you may have received from community. I will invite you to consider positive messages later in this chapter. This is an invitation to consider what the white supremacy culture has told you about who you are based on being a person of color.

Note: The self-system can be used to explore other types of internalized inferiority—for example, internalized sexism, homophobia, ableism, ageism, transphobia, and so on. For now I ask that you focus on race, and if, in the future, you would like to explore other internalizations, I encourage you to do so. Often we are responding to many types of internalized oppression at the same time.

Dismantling Racism Works understands that "there is no insulation or escape from the messages. The messages affect our individual and collective psyche despite the affirmations we may receive at home and/or in our communities."[3]

What messages have I received from the white supremacy culture about who I am based on my racial identity?

Consider messages you have received from family, given or chosen, friends, the media, the educational system, any institutions you have to now interact with or interacted with as a child, faith community, and so on.

You can replicate the diagram in figure 3.2, where the arrows represent the messages we internalize about who we are on the basis of our race. Write down the messages you have internalized from the white supremacy culture. After you have done this, take a moment to look at the messages. Take time to breathe into your body and notice how you feel physically, emotionally, mentally, and spiritually. Record any sensations, thoughts, and emotions.

Figure 3.3 represents the imbalance that happens in our self-system as a result of internalized racial inferiority. As BIPOC people, we are consistently taking in negative messages about who we are based on race, and various things manifest, including but not limited to confusion, self-doubt, self-hate, addiction, anger, apathy, anxiety, post-traumatic stress disorder (PTSD), depression; physical health issues such as hypertension, diabetes,

FIGURE 3.3

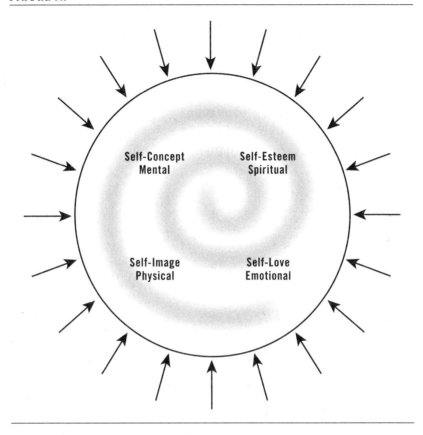

heart disease, PTSD; and denial, colorism, shame, assimilation, rage, protectionism, and invisibility. We might find ourselves engaging in behaviors that numb us so we do not have to feel our emotions connected to the racial trauma we experience because of the system of white supremacy. The image shows an imbalanced self-system because "the process of internalization is like a coil that spirals inward to the psyche. The attack on our psyches is ongoing and repetitive. As a result, our self-concept, how we see ourselves becomes limited. Our self-esteem is lowered and corrupted. Our self-image is negated and our self-love is absent."[4]

What manifests in me personally as a result of internalized racial oppression?

Please take a moment to revisit the messages you consistently take in about being a person of color according to the white supremacy culture. Reflect on what manifests for you because of white supremacy's ongoing and consistent attack on your very being due to your racial identity. Write down physical ailments or diseases, emotions that arise, thoughts and thinking patterns, descriptors of your mental state, and how your spirit has been affected because of white supremacy's relentless drive to make you feel inferior as a person of color. Once you complete your reflection, take a moment to breathe into your body and notice how you feel.

What manifests in my community?

The reflections I have invited you to engage with have been based on individual experiences of internalized racial oppression. We as BIPOC people come from communities of color, so now, I would like for you to reflect on the community of color you are from and to think about what you have experienced and witnessed in your community as a result of internalized racial oppression, such as the following:

- What does self-doubt look like when embodied within your community?
- What does self-hate look like when embodied within your community?
- How does your community express rage and grief associated with having been made invisible by a white supremacy culture?
- What has manifested in your community because white supremacy has had its knee on the community's neck for centuries?

If you are multiracial and come from two or more different communities of color, you are invited to reflect on each of these communities or the communities that feel most resonant as you answer the journaling prompts and write down your responses to them.

If you are biracial, white, or a Person of Color, you are invited to reflect on the messages you have received from the community of color from which you come. If you would like to consider messages you have internalized about being white-bodied, please reflect on and write down messages you have received about superiority based on whiteness and how white supremacy operates.

How does internalized racial oppression affect us intraracially and interracially?

Internalized racial oppression not only harms our minds, bodies, spirits, hearts, and psyches, and affects our emotional state; it also affects how we treat other BIPOC people. We not only internalize negative messages about ourselves and the communities we come from based on our racial identities; we also internalize negative messages about other groups of People of Color, which potentially leads us to replicate oppression by excluding, exploiting, or enacting violence on other BIPOC people. The only force and system that thrives when we as People of Color are oppressing one another is white supremacy.

I have seen us oppress one another interpersonally, institutionally, and culturally because of how internalized racial oppression has affected us. At times, I have given into the bias that Black people—and in particular Black men—are dangerous, and I've either crossed the street to avoid passing a Black man or I've locked my car doors if I feel as if a Black man is a little too close to my car. While I haven't consciously perpetuated stereotypes about people of Asian descent or Latinx people, I am sure I have unconsciously perpetuated stereotypes of people from different racial and ethnic groups, and there have been times in my life when I have stayed silent as my Black family members have stereotyped people from different racial and ethnic groups. I have colluded with the system of white supremacy to get funding for organizations that had not yet done the work of building relationships with communities of color.

I have witnessed BIPOC people collude with the system of white supremacy within organizations by disassociating from other BIPOC people and pandering to white-bodied people and white supremacy. At times, I have seen BIPOC people in leadership positions within organizations overlook other BIPOC people for promotions or opportunities for advancement and growth. I have observed BIPOC people upholding the characteristics of white supremacy behavior such as perfectionism, workaholism, worship of the written word, the belief there is only one right way, and power hoarding.

I have witnessed other BIPOC people stay silent about how racism is affecting People of Color within their organization. I have observed BIPOC people protecting white people at the expense of themselves and other People of Color within the organization or community. As I write about the ways in which we can oppress each other, I am not in a place of judgment against myself, and I am not asking that you judge yourself or that you judge the people who might participate in the affinity group space you will facilitate. The purpose of sharing these examples is for you to consider how you have perpetuated oppression against people who share your racial identity and those who don't.

- How has what you have internalized about the community of color you come from affected how you treat other People of Color who share your racial identity?
- What messages have you internalized about communities of color other than your own?
- How have you perpetuated oppression against communities of color other than your own by excluding, exploiting, or enacting violence physically, emotionally, mentally, spiritually, or psychically?
- How did it make you feel to reflect on these questions?

Write down your responses to these questions. These are important questions for you to consider and revisit over time in your own journey of healing due to how white supremacy has harmed you but also because you will be facilitating a space for BIPOC people to process not only what has manifested for them personally as a result of internalized racial oppression but also to process how we are treating each other intra- and interracially.

In this chapter, you have been invited to reflect on the messages you have internalized about yourself, your community, and other People of Color from the white supremacy culture. In large part, affinity spaces are designed to explore the impact of racialized trauma and internalized racial oppression and to create a space for healing our hearts, minds, spirits, and bodies. In spite of all we have internalized, it is possible and necessary for us to heal and expunge the negative messages that have taken up residence in our cells and tissues.

INTERNALIZATION AND INTEGRATION

Internalization and integration are not the same things. We internalize negative messages about who we are based on race and other identities we embody that are less proximal to power, but we do not have to fully integrate the messages and allow them to define who we are. Often there are people in our lives who serve as counterpoints to the white supremacy culture and the toxic messages it generates about BIPOC people. The purpose of understanding what we have internalized from the white supremacy culture using the self-system framework is to help us discard the mistruths about who we are and to heal from the racialized trauma we endure.

Despite the negative messages I have received from the white supremacy culture about what it means to be Black, I have pride because I am Black. While my family struggled to heal itself while reckoning with the messages they internalized from the white supremacy culture about being Black, they worked to affirm my very being by sharing messages with me about how beautiful, whole, intelligent, and brave I am. My mother, Clara, always told me my potential was limitless. My grandmother, Dorothy, squeezed me every time she saw me, offering a warm hug that communicated with my heart and let me know I was everything I needed to be and had been made in the image of God in her eyes.

The Black guidance counselor at the elementary school I attended took a special interest in me because he understood something about the experience of being the only one or one of a few BIPOC people. He understood how isolating it could be for a BIPOC person to try to be who they truly are in a sea of whiteness and an ocean of massive waves that were only meant to knock down those of us who are seen as inferior. In high school, the Latinx counselor I saw, Dr. Torres, shared the medicine from his Peruvian culture with me as a way of showing me that healing could happen in various ways, not just based on whiteness or white standards. In college and graduate school, there was an entire network of BIPOC faculty and staff who became the safety net for so many of the BIPOC students.

Even though I have received negative messages about my very being based on race from the time I was born up until now, I have had BIPOC people in my life who have affirmed that there was no need to apologize for being who I am. I have had BIPOC people in my life who have supported me in building the fortitude to challenge white supremacy. To this day I rely on affinity spaces and the People of Color I love to remind me of who I am: Black, brilliant, beautiful, divine, and sacred. It is important for us to remember who we are and to find pride in ourselves because we are BIPOC: brilliant, beautiful, divine, and sacred beings. There is most certainly some part of us that white supremacy doesn't get to define, taint, or control. We do not have to explain our reason for being. We simply need to have the space to be who we are.

> "My fullest concentration of energy is available to me only when I integrate all the parts of who I am, openly, allowing power from the particular sources of my living to flow back and forth freely through all my different selves, without the restrictions of externally imposed definition."
>
> —AUDRE LORDE, "Age, Race, Class, and Sex:
> Women Redefining Difference"

To close out this chapter, I invite you to consider the affirming and positive messages you received from BIPOC people in your life (in the next chapter we will explore how to bring together all of the content presented thus far). Remembering positive and affirming messages we have received from others is a tool I use in affinity spaces and is a tool that is grounding for me and bolsters me as I hold space for affinity groups. You can bring in messages you received from people known to you or unknown. People you have met or people you wish to meet someday. These can be artists, musicians, family members, poets, friends, or people from your faith community.

- What positive and affirming messages have you received from other BIPOC people about yourself and racial identity?
- What positive and affirming messages have you received from other BIPOC people about the community of color you come from?
- What positive messages have you received about other groups of People of Color?

"I need to see my own beauty and to continue to be reminded that I am enough, that I am worthy of love without effort, that I am beautiful, that the texture of my hair and that the shape of my curves, the size of my lips, the color of my skin, and the feelings that I have are all worthy and okay."

—TRACEE ELLIS ROSS, actress, singer, producer, and director, quoted in Ashley Weatherford, "Tracee Ellis Ross Wants to Make TV That Reflects Black People's Real Lives," *The Cut*, March 18, 2016

"You are not lucky to be here. The world needs your perspective. They are lucky to have you."

—JOSÉ ANTONIO TIJERINO, president and CEO of the Hispanic Heritage Foundation, quoted on Kipp: Chicago Public Schools, https://kippchicago.org/culture-celebrations /latinx-heritage-month-2020-celebration-highlights/, 2020.

"I stand for our cultural futures and our collective liberation—that is our indigenous cultures, our lives and our innate beauty."

—CHE SEHYUN, artist, quoted on *Public Health Insider*, https://publichealthinsider.com/2021/01/11/local-artists -depict-impacts-of-covid-19-and-racism/, November 1, 2021.

"The goal is we just want to be alive. . . . It's a fight that's holistic, it's about loving ourselves, loving the land, loving our people."

—JOAN PHILLIP, longtime Indigenous activist, member of the SnPink'tn (Penticton Indian Band), Syilx Territory, quoted on West Coast Environmental Law, https:// www.wcel.org/blog/indigenous-activism-in -canadas-past-present-and-future, July 1, 2020.

CHAPTER 4

ANTI-BLACKNESS AND THE MYTH OF RACE

*Race is a myth, but a myth with teeth and claws. Institutions, structures,
beliefs, and narratives have been created around it. Until we recognize
it for the collective delusion it is, it might as well be real.*

—RESMAA MENAKEM, *My Grandmother's Hands*

C HAPTER 3 EXPLORED internalized racial oppression, and you were invited
to investigate the messages you have internalized from dominant culture, a white supremacy culture, about your racial identity. This chapter
will explore the construct of race, racial hierarchy, and anti-Blackness. As
explained in the "Shared Language" section of chapter 1, the concept of
race itself was made up, but as Resmaa Menakem so aptly reminds us, "It
has teeth and claws and might as well be real."[1] Often, I share these ideas
with groups that race was made up and has real power. Our racialized
identities define how we move through the world, how the world experiences us, and how the world makes up meaning about our character and
who we are.

THE MYTH OF RACE

When I attended my first dismantling racism training, the facilitators
shared the History of the Race Construct as well as the racial hierarchy.
They said that there was no biological basis for race and that it had in
fact been constructed by white men of property to uphold white people
as superior, Black people as the most inferior, and other People of Color
between the two bookends of the hierarchy, Black and white. When this
was explained to me, I already knew there wasn't a biological basis for
race and that what I had learned in elementary and middle school—that
skin tone, ethnicity, and race were the same—was false. Until I attended

FIGURE 4.1

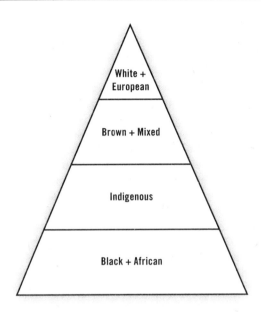

my first dismantling racism training, I didn't know how meticulously constructed race had been throughout history or how it was purposefully constructed as a hierarchy that intentionally placed Black people at the bottom of the hierarchy and other People of Color above Black and below white (see figure 4.1).

Race was constructed for social and political reasons. Two of the most pressing social and political issues of the day when race was constructed in America were colonization and the attempted genocide of Indigenous people and the enslavement of Africans. In elementary school, I learned that Columbus discovered the Americas. I remember something feeling off inside me when my teachers told me this information. I had a feeling of dissonance because somewhere in my family there was a myth that we were not only African but also Indigenous or Native American. There was a tale my grandmother would tell, about how her mother, my great-grandmother, Hopi, was part Native American. To this day I do not know if this is true. I have a picture of Hopi, and some of her facial features do look more Native American than my grandmother's or mine, but her skin is also dark, and to me she looks Black. Later in life I learned that there were many Black families who told their families the same tale my grandmother told us, that they had Native American or Indigenous heritage and ancestry.

Upon learning about Columbus and thinking about Hopi, I knew that Indigenous people were here well before Columbus arrived and claimed to have discovered their land. I was confused about why my teacher would tell me something different. The dissonance I felt about the truth and a false truth being presented to me and my classmates intensified when I was told that the Pilgrims and Indians got along and had Thanksgiving dinner together. Something in me knew that the relationship between the Pilgrims and Indians wasn't copacetic. My dissonance grew when we would play cowboys and Indians, read children's books about Pocahontas or even visit Pocahontas State Park, near my home in Richmond, Virginia. I knew women were not treated well in the 1600s, and I couldn't imagine Pocahontas willingly marrying John Rolfe. I was confused when our teachers would use historical dates as a basis for making art projects by asking us to make Indian headdresses around the time of Thanksgiving. Something felt so wrong about cutting out feathers from construction paper, placing them on a band, and wrapping it around my head. As my teacher spoke the words about Columbus discovering America, and as we were asked to comply with white supremacy and celebrate Columbus, I knew that my teacher was lying and that we were being asked to do something very violent and wrong. I knew we were being asked to erase history and to deny reality.

Columbus did come to the Americas, but he didn't discover them. Indigenous peoples had inhabited the Western Hemisphere for tens of thousands of years prior to Columbus's arrival. Upon his arrival, Indigenous people immediately experienced the colonizers' desire to dominate them through violence, including the theft of land, resources, and traditions. They experienced an attempted cultural genocide at the hands of colonizers, and this resulted in Indigenous people being left off the racial hierarchy. The colonizers who constructed the racial hierarchy tried to erase Indigenous people through a process of forced assimilation because "white" people believed Indigenous people were savage and needed to be controlled and elevated to white standards.

A horrific history that continues to reveal itself now includes the opening of the first federally sanctioned training school. In the late 1870s, a US Army veteran, Charles Pratt, opened the first federally sanctioned boarding school, the Carlisle Industrial Training School, in Pennsylvania. His philosophy was "kill the Indian, save the child" and to "elevate" Indigenous people to white standards through a process of forced assimilation. Indigenous children were taken away from their land, traditions, families, customs, and culture. They were brought to the training school by train and given a haircut and an English name and were forbidden to speak their native language. These children were taught that their Indigenous way of life was savage and inferior.

The Carlisle Industrial Training School and other schools like it initiated a pattern of abuse, including sexual and physical abuse, that continued throughout the school's history into the 1930s. Indigenous people having been left off of the racial hierarchy has resulted in the invisibilization of Indigenous people. The narrative that Indigenous people's culture is dead is directly connected to the history of forced assimilation at the hands of colonizers, white-bodied people, and the system of white supremacy. The generational and embodied trauma from a history of colonization, broken treaties, and attempted genocide continues to pervade Indigenous communities. This is trauma that is held in the body and in the entire self-system, and this takes time to heal. Healing is happening not only for the present generations but also past generations.

"Upon suffering beyond suffering: the Red Nation shall rise again and it shall be a blessing for a sick world. A world filled with broken promises, selfishness, and separations. A world longing for light again. I see a time of Seven Generations when all the colors of mankind will gather under the Sacred Tree of Life and the whole Earth will become one circle again."

—CRAZY HORSE, Oglala Sioux chief, quoted in "7th Generation,"
The Red Road Project, https://redroadproject.com/7th-generation/

Next, I will share a few points from history to show how the race and the racial hierarchy was constructed. These points are located on the Dismantling Racism Works website, www.dismantlingracism.org. This history combines the work of many scholars and historians who have researched how race was constructed and what the impact of the racial construct was throughout time. This is a very small sampling of history to illustrate how race was constructed.

The construction of race in North America was heavily influenced by racial theories created in Europe and dates back to the 1520s. Paracelsus, a Swiss physician, developed the theory of polygenism, "stating that God created the white race as superior as part of a hierarchy of races." Polygenism "created an attitude towards ethnic groups that supported the emergence of scientific racism, the pseudoscientific belief that empirical evidence exists to support or justify racism."[2]

In 1640, three servants working for a farmer named Hugh Gwyn run away to Maryland. One is described as a Dutchman, the other a Scotsman; the third is described as a Negro. They are captured in Maryland and returned to Jamestown, where the court sentences all three to thirty lashes—a severe punishment even by the standards of seventeenth-century Virginia. The Dutchman and the Scotsman are sentenced to an additional four years of servitude. But, in addition to the whipping, the Black man, named John Punch, is ordered to "serve his said master or his assigns for the time of his natural Life here or elsewhere."[3]

This historical event is very important to and influential in setting up a racial hierarchy that placed Black people at the bottom. The term "white" was not yet in use when the three servants were captured, but privilege based on nationality was playing out: the Dutchman and Scotsman were given lesser sentences than John Punch, the man described as a Negro.

The first enslaved Africans who were brought to North America had been enslaved by the Portuguese. They were brought to European colonies to what would become the United States of America. Negro means "black" in both the Spanish and Portuguese languages and is derived from the Latin word *niger*, also meaning "black." The two servants who ran away with John Punch were described by their nationalities, Dutch and Scottish, which associated with each man a geographic location and place of origin. When a person or group of people has a geographic location assigned to them, culture is also assigned. Culture is often expressed through language, customs, traditions, food, dance, rituals, and other activities. Culture and place of origin are connected with one's humanity and ability to be seen as human because their very being can be clearly traced back to a particular group of people and a place.

John Punch, the man described as a Negro, wasn't assigned a geographic location or place of origin. He was simply described by the color of his skin. This is important to understand and points to why Black people were placed at the bottom of the hierarchy. John Punch's humanity was taken away because, in essence, he was placeless. When one's humanity is taken away this becomes a justification for the person's being treating inhumanely. We are reckoning with the legacy of how John Punch was treated and the sentence he had to endure, which was to be enslaved and serve his said master for the time of his natural life here or elsewhere. He was sentenced to servitude for life. Often, Black people are seen as servants. Black people have been positioned by the white supremacy culture to take care of, clean up after, suckle the babies of, and shine the shoes of white-bodied people. We are the janitors, cafeteria workers, and domestic workers. The desire for the white supremacy culture to continue to enslave Black people and treat us inhumanely is baked into the foundation of how America became America. This is not to say that other groups of People of Color have not and are not experiencing white supremacy's attempts to enslave bodies of color; it is to say Black people were sentenced to enslavement the moment the court sentenced John Punch to be enslaved for his natural life here or elsewhere. It is to say that it is difficult to shift the cultural belief and paradigm that Black people are meant to serve white people. Although the word "white" was not yet in use when John Punch was sentenced, in 1680 the Virginia House of Burgesses began to use "white" in its laws. Prior to this time, white-skinned people were described by nationality.

The institution of science played an integral part in building the construct of race and the racial hierarchy.

> In the late 1700s, the scientific community in Europe was creating the "Oids" Theory—a race theory relying heavily upon craniometry (measurement of the brain and skull) to develop four distinct races. The science claims that the larger the brain, the higher the intelligence. Those supposed to have the largest brains, and thus to be the smartest, are the Caucasoids (where our racial designation of Caucasian comes from), next is the Mongoloid (referencing "yellow" people and those of Asian descent), Australoid (signifying "red or brown" people), and Negroid, the lowest and the only category without a geographic location. These scientific theories find their way west and begin to form a basis for the legal and cultural construction of race.[4]

As these scientific theories began to find their way west, slavery advocates turned to scientific and biblical arguments to "prove" that Negroes are distinct and inferior. Samuel Morton, the first famous American scientist, possessed the largest skull collection in the world. Using the Oids theories developed in Europe, he claimed that the larger skulls of Caucasians gave them "decided and unquestioned superiority over all the nations of the earth." Those said to have the smallest skulls and who were placed at the bottom of the hierarchy were Negroids—Black people—and the assumption was that Black people were not intelligent, which continues to shape how Black children experience the education system in the US today.

Other People of Color are situated between the two fixed points of the hierarchy, white and Black. People of Asian descent, Latinx people, and other People of Color move between the two fixed points of white and Black according to what is happening culturally and politically. The myth of the model minority was created to force people of Asian descent to assimilate and live up to white standards as well as to pit people of Asian descent against Black people.

Prior to the occurrence of 9/11, when two planes crashed into the Twin Towers in New York City, Arab people were situated close to white on the racial hierarchy. The moment the planes crashed, Arab, Arab American, Muslim people, and people perceived to be Muslim moved down the hierarchy closer to Black. Jennie Lebowitz, in her paper "Muslim American Youth in the Post 9/11 Public Education System," reports that "Islamophobia drastically increased as Muslims, Arab Americans and other citizens of Middle Eastern descent took the blame for a catastrophic event in which they played no role."[5] She notes that the Federal Bureau of Investigation states,

> Between 2000 and 2007 the rate at which the Muslim population experienced violent acts of discrimination increased by 1,600% . . . . Ostracized, the group is targeted not only by their peers, but by political and popular media as well; "othered" for their beliefs, culture and way of life. Acts of prejudice are present in all aspects of American society, including the public education system. Middle Eastern youth experience varying levels of discrimination on a daily basis, whether it be in the form of social interactions with their peers and educators, or

via government policies and popular media. As a result, Middle Eastern youth experience a hyphenated self; unable to completely identify with either their current American homeland, or the Middle Eastern home their families left behind.

In 2019, when COVID-19 emerged and government leaders across the globe began to directly and indirectly encourage hate crimes, racism, or xenophobia by using anti-Chinese rhetoric, people of Asian descent moved down in the hierarchy. Anti-Chinese rhetoric resulted in the increase of racist attacks: "By late April 2020, a coalition of Asian-American groups in the U.S. reported receiving almost 1,500 reports of incidents of violence and intimidation. Human Rights Watch reported that Asians and people of Asian descent reported attacks and beatings, violent bullying, threats, racist abuse, and discrimination linked to the pandemic across the globe."[6]

All People of Color are haunted by the history of the race construct and the racial hierarchy. We are all navigating a culture that teaches us we are less than and inferior. We all experience systemic racism, but the history of how race was constructed and our location on the racial hierarchy situate us differently; thus we experience systemic racism differently. The history we have been through as BIPOC people lives in our bodies and affects how we perceive ourselves and other BIPOC people. The hierarchy affects how we relate to each other as BIPOC people. It influences our experience of internalized racial oppression and inferiority and makes us believe other People of Color are inferior. The hierarchy contributes to the impact of internalized racial oppression on us intra- and interracially.

It is important for you as a facilitator of BIPOC affinity groups to understand the racial hierarchy and the impact it might have on the group you are facilitating. It is important for you as a facilitator of a BIPOC affinity space to understand the tension of race having been constructed and the experience of racism you and People of Color you will hold space for are having due to the racial hierarchy and the white supremacy culture in which we live. Among the common challenges that arise in BIPOC affinity groups is one dynamic I want to address that directly manifests from Black being intentionally placed at the bottom of the racial hierarchy, and that is anti-Blackness (more common challenges that arise are discussed in chapter 9).

ANTI-BLACKNESS

Anti-blackness is one way some black scholars have articulated what it means to be marked as black in an anti-black world. It's more than just "racism against black people." That oversimplifies and defangs it. It's a theoretical framework that illuminates society's inability to recognize our humanity—the disdain, disregard and disgust for our existence.

—KIHANA MIRAYA ROSS, "Call It What It Is: Anti-Blackness," *New York Times*, June 4, 2020

In 2020, many of us watched and felt the world shift in a way that most certainly confirmed we are not a post-racial society.

We were reminded of a history of Black bodies being controlled, maimed, and extinguished. On February 23, 2020, a young Black man, Ahmaud Arbery, was out on a run and was chased down and cornered by three white men (one of whom was a former police officer), who shot and killed him. On March 13, 2020, a young Black woman, Breonna Taylor, was asleep in her apartment when she was shot six times by a police officer. On May 25, George Floyd, a Black man, felt the weight of a white police officer's knee on his neck and back for nine minutes and twenty-nine seconds, until he was overwhelmed by the pressure and perished in the street. Derek Chauvin's power and posture as he knelt on George Floyd's body displayed the racial hierarchy almost too perfectly. Derek Chauvin's body looked as if it was being uplifted as he put the entire weight of his body, his internalized conviction of white superiority, and his white rage onto George Floyd. He pressed down and was uplifted in response and in real time, as this tragedy was being recorded and witnessed by so many, he illustrated the two bookends of the racial hierarchy, white on top and Black on the bottom.

KU KLUX
They took me out
To some lonesome place.
They said, "Do you believe
In the great white race?"

I said, "Mister,
To tell you the truth,

I'd believe in anything
If you'd just turn me loose."

The white man said, "Boy,
Can it be
You're a-standin' there
A-sassin' me?"
They hit me in the head
And knocked me down.
And then they kicked me
On the ground.

A klansman said, "Nigger,
Look me in the face —
And tell me you believe in
The great white race."

—Langston Hughes[7]

In my experience, and in most contexts and settings I have been in, my Blackness has been the biggest threat to whiteness. Black people are an affront to white-bodied people because we are here. We survived their attempts to enslave our bodies, minds, hearts, and spirits. And if we are thriving, this is a bigger threat and often incites white rage and violence. And if we are compassionate toward white-bodied people despite white supremacy—a system all white people benefit from but not all in the same way, and a system that has never been compassionate toward us—this can confuse white-bodied people and at times incite resentment because we are able to see white-bodied people's humanity even when they are unable to see ours. And if we are "articulate" and can speak circles around white-bodied people about white supremacy and how it affects us all, this can make white-bodied people see us as uppity or as if we are better than them. And if it is perceived that we think we are better than white-bodied people, this disrupts the entire racial hierarchy that has conditioned white-bodied people to believe they are superior and that we are the most inferior beings on the planet.

Because of the way the racial hierarchy was constructed, we have all been conditioned to believe that Black is the most inferior constructed racial identity, and there is deep healing to be done between Black people and other People of Color because of the fracture white supremacy has created in manifesting anti-Blackness. In affinity spaces, this can create some interesting and occasionally harmful dynamics. At times the feelings of Black people are disregarded when we express how our experience of systemic racism is different than that of other People of Color. I have encountered non-Black People of Color who are unable to hold this nuance in BIPOC affinity groups. Sometimes there is a desire by people who are non-Black to neutralize our experience as if we are all having the same experience of systemic racism when we are not. At other times, it can be difficult to unify the group as People of Color because of how we each experience systemic oppression and racism differently. As I described in chapter 3, I have experienced a replication of oppression in affinity groups because of internalized oppression and, at times, specifically because of anti-Blackness and how it may emerge within a particular BIPOC affinity group.

> "Black people are at once despised and also a useful counterpoint for others to measure their humanness against. In other words, while one may experience numerous compounding disadvantages, at least they're not black."
> —KIHANA MIRAYA ROSS, "Call It What It Is: Anti-Blackness," *New York Times*, June 4, 2020

I invite you as an aspiring or current facilitator of BIPOC affinity groups to consider the following:

- If you are Black, what has your experience of anti-Blackness been?
- If you are not Black, how have you been conditioned to be anti-Black?
- If you are not Black, how has anti-Blackness affected your relationship with Black people?
- How might you as a facilitator of BIPOC affinity groups handle or respond to anti-Blackness if it arises in an affinity group you are leading?

I have facilitated and participated in affinity groups for Black people and BIPOC affinity groups. I have also facilitated groups that began as

BIPOC affinity groups and then decided to split BIPOC affinity groups by race or ethnicity, given the cultural and political moment we as People of Color were experiencing. After the murder of George Floyd, I led a retreat called Healing in Community. It was a racially mixed group, with whites, People of Color, and mixed-roots or biracial people. We came together to explore the connection between grief and liberation.

We met in affinity groups for two of our sessions, and in one of the sessions we decided to have Black, biracial, non-Black People of Color, and white affinity groups. The tenderness the Black people were feeling in the group was palpable, and we needed to process in a space on our own because we were holding the gravity of the moment in a different way than any other people who attended the retreat. We knew that George Floyd could have been our father, brother, son, or uncle. We knew that if circumstances had been different, Breonna could have been one of us. We knew Ahmaud should have been able to go for a run and run freely. We understood these things in a way that other People of Color couldn't. As a facilitator in the space, I wanted to be responsive to what the group needed and make space for the specific tenderness I and the Black people in attendance were feeling. An attendee of the retreat, Celesté, who happens to be a facilitator of affinity spaces for Latinx folks, heard the request for Black folks to meet in a separate space from other folks of color and volunteered to lead the affinity space for non-Black People of Color.

In the retreat that we had, when I heard the request in the room for the Black folks who were a part of that retreat, wanting to just have their own space to me, I was like, absolutely. That makes 100 percent sense. And I wanna be a part of supporting that. . . . If I remember correctly, there were folks of Asian descent and a couple of Latinx folks in the affinity group I held. It was really beautiful what emerged in our conversation. We talked about our experiences around feeling kind of aimless because sometimes in affinity space or racial equity work conversations can be really staunch in the racial binary and hierarchy. There was some grief about not having the opportunity to further relationships and build connections with Black folks in that moment. But I think beyond that, what was helpful was to hear some commonalities and shared experiences that we had of being in this in-between space of the racial hierarchy and binary, we as non-Black People of Color embody.

—CELESTÉ MARTINEZ

Because of the racial hierarchy, anti-Blackness, and the ways racism is enacted against Black bodies, at times it makes sense to have a Black affinity group and for other races and ethnicities to meet together or separately by race or ethnicity. In the all-Black affinity group, the group might explore our specific experience of systemic racism due to being at the bottom of the racial hierarchy and the ways that is a very different experience than being white-passing or white-adjacent.

When I am in racially mixed space, spaces with white and BIPOC folks, it's like when I had to wear a business suit with pantyhose. Everything is constricted. When I am in a multiracial space, I still have on the business suit, but the pantyhose aren't there and I feel a little less constrained but still guarded. When I am in an all-Black space, I feel like I'm bathed in silk, shoes off, in my flow. I'm free.

—JEANINE T. ABRAHAM

My friend Lisa Anderson, who does affinity work with Black women, speaks about why it is her work to create healing space for Black women. While she works across lines of difference in many ways, she prioritizes the needs of Black women in her work in direct response to the racial hierarchy and her own identity and experience as a Black woman.

I just think of Toni Morrison. What she said about us being unloved. They [white-bodied people] don't love us. So we have to love us. And it is not to say there's no love for people except Black people. I don't believe that. I don't believe that the world needs to be only populated with Black folks and that it'll be heaven if it was. I don't believe that; I'm not trying to solve for that. I'm love. What does it mean to practically invest in us [Black women] as beloved?

—LISA ANDERSON

Affinity groups might be broken down by race and ethnicity in order to explore the specific experience of systemic oppression that a group of People of Color who share the same race or ethnicity might be having. For example, it might make sense to break into affinity groups of Latinx, Asian, Southeast Asian, Black African people, or Black African American people. This will depend on the context in which the affinity group is taking place—within a community, organization, faith community, or school, and with and the people in attendance. It will also depend on the purpose of the affinity group. Is the affinity group meeting to organize around an issue that affects Black people but that could use the support of other People of Color? Is the affinity group meeting to organize around an issue affecting Latinx people and division between Latinx people and Black people? Are organizational dynamics affecting all People of Color working within the organization similarly and is the affinity group meeting to address institutional racism? Is the affinity group meeting to build solidarity between different groups of People of Color in the community or in an organization?

In chapter 6, I explore facilitation skills, and in chapter 7, I dive into cultivating the skill of facilitating intuitively and being responsive to the group and what is needed. This includes knowing when to check in with a BIPOC affinity group to see if some other configuration of affinity groups needs to take place. For now, what I will offer is that it is a delicate practice to hold BIPOC affinity spaces. As People of Color we have been set up to oppress one another because a hierarchy based on bogus science classified us in different places, but we are all below white. In so many ways we are trying to claw our way up a hierarchy that will never allow us to transcend the legacy of white supremacy and the racial hierarchy. This book is offered as a resource so we do not scratch each other along the way; so we do not replicate the oppressive actions of white supremacy—a made-up system of superiority that says white people are superior and everyone else is inferior. Even though the system of white supremacy has conditioned white-bodied people to dismiss our humanity as People of Color, affinity groups give us the opportunity to see our humanity. We must work to see our humanity if we want to heal and thrive.

> "I refuse to accept the view that mankind is so tragically bound to the starless midnight of racism and war that the bright daybreak of peace and brotherhood can never become a reality. . . . I believe that unarmed truth and unconditional love will have the final word."
>
> —REVEREND DR. MARTIN LUTHER KING JR., acceptance speech, Nobel Peace Prize, Oslo, December 10, 1964

CHAPTER 5

HOW WE BEGIN

The beginning is the most important part of the work.

—PLATO

SOME TIME AGO, I participated in a training for facilitators, and someone
in the training said something like "How you begin something determines how it goes." This struck me because when I heard it, it rang so
true. The way we begin a process sets the tone for how it will go and often
determines the outcome and where we will land at the end of a process.
We can change the tone and shift course as we facilitate our affinity spaces,
and it is essential to take time to put care into how we set up and begin
facilitating an affinity group.

SET AND INTENTION

Part of preparing to begin a process involves gaining clarity about the
purpose of the process and the reasons one wants to be involved in a
particular process or project. My dear friend and colleague Stephanie
Ghoston Paul always invites individuals to consider their reason for wanting to create a new project or become involved in specific work. She asks
people to contemplate their "why" as a means of support in getting clear
about the purpose behind their desire or the actions they wish to take.
She also informs individuals that different things might move them away
from fully aligning with their why, and she urges individuals to consider
what might bring them back to it.

If you are already a BIPOC affinity group facilitator or are space-holder
who is contemplating the new role of BIPOC affinity group facilitator, it

N

is essential for you to gain clarity about your why. I recognize that some of you may work in organizations and may have been tasked with leading an affinity group. If this is the case, it is still important for you to consider your why and also how you want to lead. To gain clarity, I move through a practice of reflection to determine my why and then come up with an intention for my work. In so many ways, the intention we set determines how we show up and how things will go; an intention is an anchor we can revisit as needed to reengage with our why.

In the following list you'll find some "reflection questions" designed to support you in getting to your why and in setting an intention for your facilitation of BIPOC affinity groups. As you reflect on the questions listed, some ideas will emerge to inform your intention as a facilitator. Please write down the ideas that emerge.

- Why do you want to facilitate a BIPOC affinity group?
- What characteristics are important for a BIPOC affinity group facilitator to embody?
- What characteristics do you embody that will support you in facilitating BIPOC affinity groups?
- What do you value about BIPOC affinity groups?
- What would you like to offer to the affinity group you facilitate?
- How do you want participants to feel in your affinity group?
- Why are you uniquely qualified and positioned to lead BIPOC affinity groups?

After you reflect on the different reflection questions, I suggest you write an intention statement, almost like a mission statement for facilitation. This can be your guiding post, your true north, and will serve as a reminder of how and why you want to facilitate BIPOC affinity groups.

For example: My intention as a BIPOC affinity group facilitator is

- To show up authentically and share about my lived experience as a Black person in a way that serves the group
- To create and co-create space with other BIPOC where we can share with one another in an authentic way that isn't limited by systems like white supremacy

- To create a space where people in the affinity group feel seen, heard, held, and healed
- Offer new skills and strategies for participants in the affinity group to implement in their work and lives
- Build and strengthen relationships between group participants
- Work to create conditions for new pathways to be forged focused on the liberation of BIPOC people.

If you choose to write an intention or mission statement, consider printing it out or writing it down so that you can revisit it each time you facilitate an affinity group.

CREATING A JOB DESCRIPTION

In addition to your why and intention, you might want to create a job description for your role as a BIPOC affinity group facilitator. A job description might also be helpful if you work in an organization or are engaged in community organizing where affinity groups are part of the organizing strategy. Your job description might depend on the context in which you are facilitating an affinity group and also on the purpose of the group. A job description for an affinity group leader could include things like setting the tone for the space by offering shared agreements or community-care practices; facilitating a process whereby group participants can explore how white supremacy, racism, and internalized oppression have affected them; offering tools focused on healing from racial trauma; supporting the group participants in building relationships with one another; creating an organizational strategy to respond to white supremacy and racism; and where applicable, working in relationship with white affinity groups to build solidarity and take collective action.

LOGISTICS OF AFFINITY GROUPS

In this section I provide more information about logistics and other issues to consider as you begin leading affinity groups.

Context

Some questions to consider concerning the context:

- Is the affinity group taking place within an organization or workplace?
- Is the affinity group a one-time training or part of a longer-term racial equity initiative?
- Are you offering an affinity group as part of a more significant organizing effort within a community?
- Is the affinity group taking place in response to a racialized experience that has occurred within an organization or community?

These are just a few things to consider. Later in this chapter I include information about how the context might determine the content you will choose to cover as you lead a BIPOC affinity group, and in chapter 8 I go into much greater detail about leading affinity groups in an organization versus in a community.

Group Attendees

There are some critical things to consider about group attendees. This information will affect the content and flow of your agenda.

RELATIONSHIPS

- Do the group participants know each other either within the context of a community or organization?
- Are the group participants only meeting one time, and are they unlikely to see each other again?
- Were affinity group participants required to attend or was it voluntary?
- Have group participants met in an affinity group in the past?
- What, if any, preexisting relationships do group members have with one another?

ACCOMMODATION OF SPECIAL REQUIREMENTS

- Do group participants need any special accommodations? For example, if you are offering an affinity group over Zoom, do you offer closed-captioning?
- If you are offering an affinity group in English and English is not the first language of some participants, do you have access to interpretation services?

- If you are offering an in-person affinity group, is the space in which you are offering it accessible for people with disabilities?
- How might you teach to different learners in the space?
- Is childcare needed for people to participate?
- Is transportation a barrier to participation?

Power Dynamics

As a seasoned facilitator, I can predict that power dynamics will emerge in a group, and I can usually feel or sense how power dynamics affect a group dynamic. Power dynamics are always present in groups. Power dynamics affect us even when we work to neutralize power. There is no neutral. We all embody identities such as race, class, gender identity and expression, sexual orientation, ability, and age, among others. These identities determine how much power we are assigned or given by dominant culture and how much power is taken away from us by systems of oppression.

It is vital to hold an intersectional lens as you facilitate. One way to do this is to remember that the multiple points of oppression we embody are compounded; each point makes us less proximal to institutional and cultural power. The points of privilege we embody also are compounded, allowing us to be more proximal to power. In addition to the points of privilege and oppression we embody, you also want to consider how positional power might impact group dynamics. For example, if you are offering an affinity group in an organization, gather as much information as possible about the group and different roles, departments, teams, and positions prior to leading the affinity group.

At the beginning of an affinity group in an organization, and during group introductions, you can ask participants to describe the various roles they fulfill at the company and how positional power works within the organization. If you are leading an affinity group in the context of a public racial equity or anti-racism training and representatives are in attendance from the same organization, you will want to know this to better understand how power dynamics may emerge as you lead the affinity group. At times, I have named how power is present in an affinity group, given the different identities participants embody and the various roles and positions that might be represented in the group. We cannot know everything about the dynamics that may present themselves as we prepare to lead an affinity group, and I find it very helpful to the process to know as much as I can prior to leading the group. Sometimes this involves creating a simple questionnaire for participants to reflect on before we meet in the group, which will provide more insight and context, and sometimes this might be a matter of my inquiring with organizational leaders or staff to gain further insight and context.

Size of an Affinity Group

I have facilitated affinity groups with as few as four participants and as many as eighty. There is no ideal size. Smaller groups feel more intimate, and it might be easier to build relationships within them. That said, I have also experienced remarkable transformation in larger affinity groups. If you know the size of the group in advance, you can prepare your agenda in a way that is responsive to the needs of a small and large group and what the goal of the affinity group is. For example, in a small group you might have time for everyone to share, but it might be challenging to make time for everyone to share in a larger group, or you might need to be creative about how people share. Sometimes with larger groups, I present content and then have people move into smaller groups to reflect or pair-share. In large or small groups, you need to be conscious of how much time individual participants in the group are taking up. You want to ensure that everyone has time to share.

Location of the Group

If you are offering an in-person affinity group, participants must feel that they are in a confidential space. If you are offering the affinity group in an organization, you will need a room that doesn't carry sound to other parts of the organization. Or you could host the affinity group off-site. If you are leading an affinity group in a building where different activities take place, to the greatest extent possible ensure that there will be no interruptions to the affinity group, such as people planning to use the room after you but who arrive early, or people interrupting your affinity group because they were unaware it was taking place.

Separating into Smaller Groups

If you are facilitating an anti-racism or racial equity training and you break up the large, racially mixed group into smaller affinity groups, it is essential to explain why we meet in affinity groups. Earlier in this book I explained why we as BIPOC people need a separate space to be with each other. If I am facilitating a racial equity training together with a white-bodied facilitator, prior to breaking into affinity groups my co-facilitator and I typically explain to participants why we are splitting into affinity groups: BIPOC people and white-bodied people have different work to do in response to white supremacy and racism. I say that we need to be in space with one another to heal from racialized trauma and how white supremacy and racism have affected us. The white-bodied facilitator explains why white-bodied individuals need to have a space to process how they have been shaped and what they have internalized from the white supremacy culture.

I am not mixed roots or biracial. If I am co-leading a larger dismantling racism initiative that includes affinity groups, when we split into affinity groups we explain why we are doing so, and we also explain that neither I nor the white co-facilitator is biracial and mixed roots. We acknowledge that we are asking biracial and mixed-roots participants to make a choice between a white or BIPOC affinity group. This is a choice that may not feel easy and yet it is a choice I ask biracial and mixed-roots folks to make in most settings in which I facilitate BIPOC affinity groups. I usually suggest that people consider how the world sees them, how they are treated because of where they fall in the racial hierarchy, or if they are white-adjacent, whether they at times choose to pass as white. I have had the experience of having people who do not identify as white but who can pass as white and biracial folks attend my affinity groups and I've had the experience of people who can pass as white and biracial people go to the white affinity group and then make their way over to the affinity group space I am facilitating.

In June 2020, I held a public affinity group for BIPOC people. My friend Sherene attended and shared the following with me:

> One of the continuously painful aspects is that because of the ambiguity of not only being mixed heritage, but being mixed heritage from the Middle East, . . . the proximity to whiteness is all over the place. Fairly recently when I went to the first affinity group you were facilitating, I was really scared to join the BIPOC group. I knew I couldn't join the white group because I knew I will make people uncomfortable in that group. I knew I couldn't go to that group. In the BIPOC affinity group, I was really afraid that I was going to be told that I didn't belong. It was a very large group and there were other people with similar heritage there.

Sherene, who lives in the North with her white husband, went on to describe some of her experience of being mixed roots and not identifying as white and why she chooses to attend BIPOC affinity groups:

> We went to Virginia for a wedding in [my husband's] family and I was walking through the hotel and everybody kept staring at me, and I mentioned it to my husband. I'm bringing my babies along and doing all sorts of stuff. And I was expecting my husband to say something like it's because you're so beautiful or something. He said, "It's because of the way you look [not white-bodied], that's why they're staring at you." I was still, like, whatever, okay. It took a long time for me to accept that the reason . . . that the experiences that I've had in my life were actually because of other people's unconscious biases. It was through affinity groups that I can say that confidently now, because when I go into these affinity groups, my experiences are more similar and recognizable among the BIPOC group.

Sherene's experiences speak to the camaraderie that can happen in BIPOC affinity groups between mixed-roots and biracial participants and those who do not identify as biracial. They also speak to the fact that some mixed-roots and biracial people find a place for themselves in a BIPOC affinity group.

I have been part of training collectives that included biracial and mixed-roots facilitators. In these collectives we would offer three affinity groups: for biracial and mixed-roots identities, for BIPOC identities, and for white identities. If you do not identify as biracial or mixed roots, please consider how you might respond to a scenario where biracial or mixed-roots people want to participate in the affinity group process. If you are biracial or mixed roots, please consider how you would lead a BIPOC affinity group and honor the experiences of those who are located lower on the racial hierarchy. This is not about perfection; it is about understanding many of the concepts already introduced. It is about understanding how our racial identities and our location on the racial hierarchy will affect our facilitation and experience of a racially mixed affinity group.

When separating into affinity groups, we are mindful of the dynamic that occurs when asking the BIPOC people in attendance to leave the space. If possible, the BIPOC people stay in the main meeting space, and the white-bodied individuals go to a separate space for their affinity group. If there are more white-bodied than BIPOC participants in the room, the BIPOC participants may be asked to move to another room. If you are also offering a mixed-roots or biracial affinity group, you will need a third meeting space. If BIPOC participants are asked to move, it is important to be transparent about why, given the history of asking us to accommodate white people and white comfort.

In-Person Versus Zoom Groups

Over the years, many of us have learned how to shift our work and offerings online. I prefer to meet in person, but this isn't always possible. If you plan to hold your affinity group over Zoom, please make sure participants understand how to mute and unmute. There may be other norms you typically establish, such as using the raised-hand function or unmuting or asking participants to unmute or type "stack" in the chat if they want to share. "Stack" originated in the Occupy movement as a way for people to comment on proposals or ask questions in public meetings. Zoom has a function for people to indicate they want to speak or be added to the queue to speak. It is also important to make sure people have space to share on Zoom. You might use breakout rooms or small groups more than usual, or you might decide to stay in the main area the entire time. Some of this will depend on the size and dynamics of the group.

Length of Session

I find that an hour is never long enough for a BIPOC affinity group—we can easily fill up ninety minutes. Some of us do not often get to be in BIPOC-only spaces, and we can feel like we never want to leave them. If you have agency over deciding the length of an affinity group, ninety minutes is a good starting point. Sometimes, when working in organizations, it is challenging to carve out ninety minutes; if this is the case, you might offer a sixty- or seventy-five-minute affinity group.

SETTING THE TONE

Now that you have more of an understanding of factors to consider as you prepare to lead an affinity group, and you're clearer about your *why* as an affinity group leader, it is important to consider practices that help set the tone for an affinity group in a way that supports the participants and the overall goal of the group.

Opening

Typically, I begin an affinity group with an opening. This usually lasts a few minutes and gives people space to arrive, breathe, and settle in. Often I lead a guided meditation for the group or offer a moment of silence to honor our transition out of one place and into another. If you aren't a trained mindfulness or yoga teacher, you can find many guided meditations and mindfulness practices online to use as a basis for your opening. My only suggestion is to practice the meditation several times on your own before offering it in a group. It is also important to credit the source of whatever mindfulness practice meditation you offer.

Some of you may feel uncomfortable with the idea of offering a moment of mindfulness and space for the nervous system to settle. It feels important to provide tools that are antidotes to white supremacy in BIPOC affinity groups. White supremacy asks us to speed up while also giving us a message that we are lazy. White supremacy promotes a grind culture in which our work and productivity levels are measures of our worth. Given the racial trauma we experience on a daily basis, it is important for us to engage in practices that allow us to slow down.

In *Pause, Rest, Be: Stillness Practices for Courage in Times of Change,* my friend Octavia Raheem gifts us with a call to pause:

Human
Be. Still.
We can no longer outrun this without collectively slowing down.
We cannot profit from this without the bottom meticulously falling out.
We cannot package, sell, or otherwise capitalize on this without paying with
    our very own lives.[1]

White supremacy comes for our souls. It tries to steal us away from ourselves and each other. A moment of rest as we enter space together, a moment of stillness as we sit with one another, and a moment of pause as we heal together feels like the perfect way to begin an affinity group, and it serves as an invitation to continue to find stillness amid the chaos of white supremacy—a system that thrives off of our backs and the trauma it inflicts upon us.

Calling Ourselves into a Space

After opening the group, I invite participants to "call themselves into the space." Much as taking a moment to open your space with a mindfulness or meditation practice is an antidote to white supremacy culture, inviting participants to call themselves into the space also serves as an antidote to white supremacy culture. Calling oneself into a space serves more than one purpose; it is a time for someone to fully presence themselves in the space and let people know who they are. It allows the group participants to begin to build relationships with one another. I ask affinity group participants to share the name they want to be called by in the space, their pronouns, and a land acknowledgment if they have one, and to respond to a prompt. The prompt could be an invitation for group participants to share a feeling, call in an ancestor they would like to be present in the space, or share something they feel grateful for. (See chapter 7 for facilitator techniques and prompts you can explore in the affinity groups you lead.)

If you have a large group, you might decide to have people break into smaller groups to introduce themselves. This also might be the only time in your group when you get to hear everyone's voice. If you are in an organization and people in the affinity group know each other, you may not need to spend as much time on making space for participants to call themselves into the space. Still, it is a nice practice to offer a prompt so people can check in with one another.

Assumptions

In chapter 1, I shared a list of assumptions that guide my anti-racism work and practice. If you are leading an affinity group and assumptions haven't been shared, you will want to take time to share some assumptions and more about your philosophy with group participants. You can share assumptions via email prior to the time of the affinity group, or you can spend a few minutes going over them at the beginning of the affinity group session. As a reminder, assumptions are not agreements; they are about what has informed your work and how you work. Assumptions are based on things you have learned and know to be true about our white supremacy culture and the way we, as BIPOC people, have to navigate the culture. Assumptions are a time to share your belief around how we arrive in a place of liberation—collective liberation for BIPOC people and all beings. They are an important part of setting the tone, and I find that assumptions are a reference point to refer back to as different dynamics surface during the affinity group.

COMMUNITY-CARE PRACTICES

Taking the time to set community-care practices, sometimes referred to as guidelines or agreements, is one of the most critical parts of leading an affinity group. I have been in spaces where we take the time to go over agreements but do not really live up to our agreements. We all agree to be respectful and then proceed to be disrespectful to one another. We all agree to confidentiality and then break confidentiality immediately after leaving a group space.

In October 2021, I was co-leading a training about facilitation, and one of the participants, Natasha Harrison, called agreements "community-care practices." This struck me because agreements really do serve as a way for us to show that we care about each other. Agreements speak to what people need in a space. They speak to the boundaries needed in any group. They are guardrails for you as the facilitator and group participants. All of these things are a matter of care. You can choose to call your guidelines agreements or community-care practices.

In affinity groups, I either co-create community-care practices with the group or suggest a short list of community-care practices. Some of this depends on the context in which the affinity group is taking place as well as on how much time has been allotted for it. If you want to co-create community-care practices with the affinity group, this will take more time than offering your list of agreements. You can let participants know that the group has ten to fifteen minutes to come up with a list of community-care practices. You can invite participants to name some community-care practices that feel important to them. You can write them on a flipchart or whiteboard if you are meeting in person with the group. If you are on Zoom, participants can type their suggested community-care practices into chat or use something like Jamboard, a Google app that allows people to type in information and add it to a document that everyone can access. Groups tend to come up with a lot of practices if given time to co-create them. You might need to categorize them by theme and create a more concise list. In my experience, the lists of community-care practices that groups co-create tend to align with the practices that I typically offer in groups, such as those that follow.

Speak from Your Experience

This practice supports a group in not generalizing individual experiences onto the entire group. I speak from my own experience by using "I" statements, and there are other ways people can share without assuming that everyone else has had the same or a similar experience.

Listen to Understand

Your goal is for participants to practice listening to what is shared and create an environment where they are listened to when they share. You can talk about listening and receiving what someone is sharing and explain how you want group participants to listen. For example, they can listen with their entire being, listen to receive the words or the sentiment someone is sharing and without needing to receive only sentiments that affirm what they believe. Listen because it is vulnerable for another person to share.

Expect and Accept Non-Closure

The work of dismantling racism is never-ending. Affinity groups rarely offer closure, and I like to let group participants know they might leave the session feeling tender, grateful, and open, and that they may have more questions at the end of the affinity group than they did at the start of it. Although a particular affinity group might have definite start and stop times, things will not be tidy, wrapped up in a bow at the end of the affinity group. It is an ongoing process to undo what we have internalized as BIPOC people, to build authentic relationships intra- and interracially, and to heal ourselves.

Intent Does Not Equal Impact

This is listed in the group of assumptions in chapter 1, and I often offer discussion of this idea as a community-care practice. Group participants need to understand that good intentions do not equal a positive impact. This knowledge allows us to offer better care to each other. As mentioned earlier, the world isn't harm-free and your affinity groups will not be harm-free zones. This practice of acknowledging intent and attending to impact is really a practice of being able to hold one another's humanity with an awareness that we have all been socialized and conditioned by systems of oppression and we must be accountable for the impact of our actions and the things we say or do in a space.

Confidentiality

When we enter into an affinity space, we enter into a sacred space. One way to uphold the sanctity of the space is to ask group participants to keep what is said in the group in the group. Another way to speak about confidentiality, particularly in the context of an organization, is to ask that there be no retribution or attribution. This is important if there are different levels of positional power in the room. Do you attribute comments to specific people who participated in the affinity group? It's important that group participants share without fear of retaliation or retribution.

Safer Space

This community-care practice speaks to the reality that we cannot create a truly safe space. A space that feels safe to someone can become unsafe within minutes. We know the world isn't safe because we are navigating a white supremacy culture that makes us feel unsafe and doesn't see the value in creating conditions for us to be safe. Instead of promising that the affinity group is a safe space, you can assure participants that you will attempt to make it a safer space—safer than dominant culture, safer than hostile work environments, safer than all of the things that get in the way of our ability to be free. Safer space is an acknowledgment that even an affinity group isn't a harm-free zone. Safer space asks us to respond when harm happens, name power dynamics that inform why and how harm happens, share vulnerably, and care for each other as we respond to how our safety has been compromised because of white dominance and supremacy.

Please consider other community-care practices you want to offer the group. You can also share this list with them and ask if they want to add anything to it.

Context and Content

If the affinity group you lead takes place within the context of a larger anti-racism or racial equity training, you might focus on processing how the training is going for participants and introduce a conversation about internalized racial oppression or further process something that came up earlier during the training. If you are leading an ongoing affinity group that meets regularly, you might decide to ask participants what would be most helpful for them to discuss during their time together in the group. They might want to discuss racial trauma, self-care, and collective care, or they might want to strategize in response to something that has come up organizationally or, if you are offering a community affinity group, something that has happened within their community. The context will determine the content, and I find that many groups aren't shy at all about what is needed and what they want to discuss. The sample agenda in this chapter will offer some ideas for what content you might want to cover, and more sample agendas will be included in the appendix.

Closing the Group

After the group moves through the content and topics you and they wished to cover in the affinity group, prepare to lead a closing activity, to signal and shape the transition out of the special space of the group. Affinity groups can open up so much for participants, and it is important to make space to close the time spent in them with intention and care. Chapter 7 focuses on facilitator techniques and prompts, and includes prompts and ideas for closing. I make sure to leave enough time for the affinity group to do another round of check-ins. They might share something related to what they appreciated about being in the affinity group or share a self-care or healing practice that supports them as they respond to racialized trauma. They might share an appreciation for someone in the group or share ways they would like to continue to receive support from the affinity group. Many of the one-session affinity groups I lead find ways to stay in community with each other. You could also close by leading another mindfulness or meditation practice, or offer a moment of silence to honor that the group is coming to a close and a transition is happening. This transition feels particularly important when you are meeting in an affinity group within the context of a racial equity or anti-racism training. There is a transition from affinity groups back into the large group, and this can feel jarring for BIPOC people. We go from a space that may have felt safer back into a space that is racially mixed. Preparing the group for this transition is important, as is setting expectations about what you will share with the large group about the experience in the affinity group.

Sometimes there are report-backs in which representatives from each affinity group share themes that emerged in the group. Other times, the affinity group facilitators take on the role of reporting back themes in the large group. If the affinity groups are taking place in an organization or community that is involved in a larger racial equity process, affinity groups may have information to report back about equity goals or an equity plan.

As groups come back together, it is important to acknowledge this transition back into the racially mixed space. I usually invite folks to breathe for a few minutes together and then open the space for report-backs, if they are taking place. If I am leading a public community training that is not part of a larger racial equity process, I have the group breathe together, and then I might ask a question like "What do you now know?" and invite individuals to share in the space for a few minutes. If there is going to be open sharing in response to a prompt or report-backs, before you open up the conversation remind the group of the agreements made earlier.

If you are leading an affinity group within an organization and people are heading back into work meetings after the affinity group ends, you will want to prepare them to transition out of the affinity group and back into work, where they might encounter some white-bodied people or colleagues. Often, I ask what people need as they transition and encourage them to take some space between the affinity group and their work demands. If this isn't possible for a participant, we might strategize about what care looks like for them amid having to encounter white-bodied people or colleagues after leaving the affinity group. (In chapter 8 I discuss in more detail the difference between leading affinity groups in organizations versus in community.)

To close this chapter, I offer a sample agenda that follows the sequence just described.

SAMPLE AGENDA *Affinity Group*

SESSION LENGTH: 90 minutes

OPENING MEDITATION AND CENTERING: 10 minutes

CALLING OURSELVES INTO THE SPACE: The length of time will depend on the size of the group. If you have 20 people, you could ask everyone to take a minute to introduce themselves. If you have more than 20 people, you could have people break into small groups to do introductions. If you are on Zoom and meeting with a large group, you might use the chat to have folks introduce themselves and then send them into smaller groups. For the purposes of this sample agenda, I will allot 20 minutes for introductions.

ASSUMPTIONS/AGREEMENTS: 10 to 15 minutes

CONTENT: You have many options for content. You can cover internalized racial oppression, racialized trauma, and the self-system, or use the time to process whatever it is the group needs most. You might deliver content for about 10 minutes and then have people move into smaller groups to share. If you have people break into smaller groups, they could come back to the large group and share themes. This entire process will take a minimum of 30 minutes.

CLOSING: 15 minutes

If you only have an hour, you can adapt the introductions and content. Please make sure to mindfully open and close the group.

CHAPTER 6

SKILLFUL FACILITATION

*Facilitation is a Black Art. Why? Because every facilitation process is
a journey into the unknown. A possible future. A bright Black field of
possibility. That's why we need facilitators as guides. Because it is not
easy to face the death of how things have been and to open up to the
vulnerability of how things could be. But we must.*

—ALEXIS PAULINE GUMBS, quoted in adrienne maree brown,
Holding Change: The Way of Emergent Strategy Facilitation and Mediation

NOTHING MOVES MY HEART and spirit more than creating and being in
circle (virtually or physically) with others who are striving to find
their way home to themselves and each other. Circles themselves represent the infinite, connection, and wholeness. Pythagoras's musing about
circles encapsulates how powerful circles can be. "As Pythagoras would
say, the circle is the most perfect shape, it withholds all, and everything
emerges out of it."[1] As a facilitator, I have the honor and privilege of
creating, co-creating, and sitting in circle with others. As a Black person
and anti-racism educator, I have the honor and privilege of creating,
co-creating, and sitting in circle with other Black people and People of
Color as we push up against and heal from the white supremacy culture
in which we live—a culture laden with toxicity that permeates the air we
are trying to breathe.

Facilitating and holding space for transformation to occur is not easy,
but, in my experience, it is often rewarding. Facilitating and holding space
for transformation changes the facilitator as much as the group they are
facilitating. This chapter explores the depths of what it means to facilitate
BIPOC affinity groups, and ultimately, how we can facilitate change and
transformation. First, it feels important to define transformation so you

have a clearer picture of what you are being tasked with as you move into the role of facilitating BIPOC affinity groups. Transformation is an alchemical process whereby we change from one state of being into another. Often it takes time, and sometimes, part of the process of moving from one state of being into another is accompanied by some discomfort, but also, in my experience, some points of ease. The BIPOC affinity spaces I have held and participated in have certainly felt uncomfortable at times, but they have also provided me a sense of ease.

SKILLS OF A FACILITATOR

As I considered what skills have supported me as a facilitator or transmitter of transformation, and what I have witnessed in other adept facilitators, the following skills rose to the top of my list:

- Self-awareness
- Patience
- Compassion
- Openness
- Excellent listening skills
- An understanding of right-timing
- How to use silence in a group
- The balance between offering structure and spaciousness
- An understanding of intersectionality
- The ability to navigate conflict
- A willingness to throw the agenda out and change course

In the next section I explore each of these skills and offer opportunities for you to reflect on your experience with each of them.

Self-Awareness

Cool means being able to hang with yourself.

—PRINCE, *Rolling Stone*

To become more aware of oneself, one has to develop a deep relationship with oneself. In my experience, relationships are often messy, especially the ones we cultivate with ourselves. To cultivate self-awareness, we have to be willing to dive into ourselves, discover how we've been shaped, and explore the patterns that have emerged from our shaping, both those that create obstacles for us and those that allow us to more fully come into alignment with our highest self and the highest good. We must be willing to turn toward the parts of ourselves we label as unworthy and unlovable. We must be willing to examine the parts of ourselves we feel aren't enough. We need to be willing to discover new aspects of ourselves. All of these things require us to be with ourselves. In so many ways, this is what we are asking affinity group participants to do—deepen self-awareness. Ayodele Harrison runs an affinity group for Black male educators and reflects on part of what he is working on himself and fostering in his affinity group and work with Black men. Ayodele also shared about the connection between self-awareness and vulnerability:

> *Part of this work and skill building is around emotional intelligence. In short, how, am I growing my awareness of myself—my awareness of myself, with other people in the space, and then being aware of what other people might be going through and growing with that? There are few formal places where Black men can deepen their understanding of emotional intelligence and engage practices that enhance it. … As a Black man myself working with cohorts of Black men, I understand that we enter in (to Black men affinity groups) with our guards up. So I create and curate affinity group spaces that invite men, who might feel guarded and nervous about showing up as their full authentic self, to share openly, engage in judgment free conversation protocols, and practice independent and community wide reflection activities as we are building our facilitative leadership skills.*

—AYODELE HARRISON

In the context of facilitating a group, and especially a BIPOC affinity group, we need to be aware of how racism has affected and is affecting us. We need to be mindful of our shaping in response to internalized racial oppression and, as much as we can, of where our pain points live and what triggers them. We need to be aware of our conditioned responses when we begin to feel off-center as we facilitate and hold space for transformation. We also need to be able to recognize when we need a break or pause.

Self-awareness is a skill we have the opportunity to continue to deepen throughout our lives. We can build self-awareness through self-reflection and study, and we can ask for feedback about our facilitation style from colleagues or friends. We can grow self-awareness through meditation,

mindfulness, and contemplative practices such as journaling and movement, including yoga, tai chi, walking or moving meditations, or doing
something creative without a goal in mind or attachment to the outcome.

- What are you currently practicing to deepen your awareness
  of yourself?
- What would you like to practice to deepen your awareness
  of yourself?
- Why is self-awareness a critical skill for a facilitator of BIPOC
  affinity spaces to possess?

Patience

Patience is not passive; on the contrary it is concentrated strength.

—BRUCE LEE, Striking Thoughts:
Bruce Lee's Wisdom for Daily Living

Cultivating a practice of patience in my life is certainly something I will
do for the rest of my life. I am a fiery Leo sun, a visionary, and according
to the Human Design framework, a Manifestor Generator. I want things
to move and move fast because I'm quite clear that we do not have time
to waste when it comes to healing ourselves and our planet.

Being a facilitator in many kinds of spaces has taught me that we cannot
rush a process. The magic of what can emerge from a group process comes
from allowing things to unfold organically and naturally. White supremacy
has taught many of us that efficiency and focusing on outcomes is more
valuable than the process we move through to get to a particular outcome.
White supremacy says productivity is more important than the process.
These beliefs have no place in processes meant to generate transformation.

When you facilitate, it is likely that things will not go exactly as you
planned. You might experience technical difficulties, people in the group
might go off on a tangent in conversation, there might be a disruption to
the group process that you cannot control, and a myriad of other things
could happen. Being patient with yourself and others while continuing to
move the group in a direction that supports the collective goal and purpose
is a critical skill to embody.

Practicing patience while facilitating might entail slowing down, pausing, or taking a deep breath. It might look like meeting people where they

are even if their understanding of racism or the impact of internalized racism is different than yours. Practicing patience while you facilitate can look like reminding the group that you all have the time you need. Undoubtedly, being patient as you facilitate means trusting yourself, the group, and the process.

- What is your relationship with the practice of patience?
- What is your growing edge as you work to fully embody the skill of being patient as you facilitate?
- Can you recall a time when patience supported a group process in a generative and positive way?

Compassion

Compassion is the radicalism of our time.

—DALAI LAMA XIV

When I first started working in social change and activist spaces focused on dismantling white supremacy, I rarely heard anything about the role of love and compassion in our work of creating conditions for our collective liberation. This confused me. I didn't understand how we could create conditions for liberation without centering love, because to me it seems that loving ourselves is the pathway we must move down if we want to get free. As time passed, my own understanding of compassion and love and my practice to develop more compassion and loving-kindness for myself and others deepened. I began to understand more about what it looked like to lovingly and compassionately call someone in or up or set a boundary. I learned more about how modeling compassion can invite people more deeply into their hearts. More was revealed to me about how compassion is key if we want to transmute that which is in the way of us being free, individually and collectively.

I am very clear that we will not make our way out of white supremacy and all of the harm it inflicts upon us by being indifferent or heartless to one another. As facilitators, we have a responsibility to be as compassionate as possible toward ourselves and others. When we cannot summon compassion for others, we can still practice extending grace to ourselves. One reason it feels important to me for facilitators in any space, and particularly a BIPOC affinity space, to cultivate compassion for self and others is because we are all fallible in perpetuating the harm that happens on our planet. None of us is above reproach. We don't know what we don't know. We all have things to learn. We all have growing edges and room to stretch into a new way of being.

Embodying compassion means knowing how deeply my heart is connected to yours—and understanding how deeply connected your heart and suffering are connected to the People of Color you will hold space for. It means telling someone the truth about their behavior if they behave in a way that harms the group you are facilitating. It means calling people into being a better version of who they are. It means calling yourself into doing the same. BIPOC affinity spaces can push up against the raw edges or tender spots you need to explore for yourself. This is why it is important to work to be more compassionate as you hold people and move people through a transformative process.

- What is your definition of compassion?
- What role do you believe compassion has in your work as a BIPOC facilitator?
- What practice(s) might support you in being more compassionate toward yourself and others?

Listening

Listening is the most difficult skill to learn
and the most important to have.

—AFRICAN PROVERB

In chapter 5, I shared information about how to set up affinity groups, including a list of community-care practices or agreements. "Listening to understand" is included in that list. In affinity groups it is important to name that many of us have not been listened to. Our experiences as BIPOC people have been discounted, denied, and silenced by white dominant culture. Some of us may also have been taught, within our own families, to listen and not speak or be seen and not be heard. This context feels important because, in so many ways, we have been begging a culture that doesn't value listening to and seeing us to do just that. The beauty of an affinity group is that we have an opportunity to be in a context where there is a shared experience of having been silenced or having had our stories and words not listened to, though sometimes in different ways, depending on our other identities apart from race. These experiences can call us into co-creating a listening practice that genuinely honors what each person is saying and sharing with us. They call us to practice making space for each person to be heard.

In my experience, I have felt listened to when a person in some way indicates they heard what I have shared with them. This can be through repeating back what I said to them to make sure they heard it in the way I intended, making eye contact or giving a nod of the head, and letting me know the person I am speaking with is present with me and not distracted by something or someone else. Many of us have been conditioned to talk but not taught how to truly listen to ourselves or others. Dominant culture conditions us to listen for whether or not what someone is communicating with us is true or false, or good or bad, or is affirming something we believe to be accurate, etc. Dominant culture has taught me that listening means I should only use my sense of hearing instead of listening with my entire body and soul. Listening is a full-bodied experience.

For me as a facilitator, listening is an essential skill. Listening is not just about hearing what someone shares; it is also about receiving what is shared, if we can, and making sure we heard it correctly. If I am not fully present or listening, I cannot track the conversation or space or the group's needs. Listening requires me to listen to what is spoken and to listen for the unspoken or for things that aren't being named. It requires me to hear the space between words and sentences. Listening for the unspoken might inspire me to ask a question of an individual in the affinity group or the group as a whole so as to draw out what I believe needs to be spoken and recognized. I listen to the words someone is sharing and, when possible, read and listen to the body language of the person sharing and of others in the affinity group. Someone sharing vulnerably about their experience with me, or even sharing something with me that might seem mundane, is a gift. Listening allows us to be present to receive this gift.

- What does it mean to listen with your entire body?
- Why is listening an important skill for an affinity group facilitator to practice and model?
- What guidelines or agreements can you put in place to invite people into a space of deep listening?

Silence

Listen to the wind; it talks. Listen to the silence;
it speaks. Listen to your heart; it knows.

—NATIVE AMERICAN PROVERB

I am a trained therapist and a mindfulness and spiritual practitioner. Both of these skills have certainly improved my comfort with silence, but the truth is, I think I have always loved silence. I love silence because it allows me to tune in and listen to myself. Not the noise in my mind but to my inner knowing and wisdom. My intuition.

White supremacy has tried to make us believe we do not know anything; it has tried to make us disconnect from our intuition and inner knowing. We are wise, especially about our own experience of oppression and what it feels like to live in a culture that doesn't want us to exist or thrive. Silence can put us back in touch with our inner wisdom and knowing. Silence can allow us to release the stories and patterns that keep us bound to a belief system that is based on a hierarchy, which ranks us and pits us against each other. Silence can allow us to take the time we need to pause and reflect on what the next right step might be. It can allow for an opening in a group and make space for voices to be heard that would not otherwise speak in a group.

For me as a facilitator, it is important to know the possible reasons silence might be present—be that because of stagnant energy in a group or because the facilitator needs to bridge and connect what individuals in the group are sharing. Silence can be generative, healing, and supportive. I can feel when a group is stuck and needs me to say something to move us through a difficult moment. I can feel when I should just let the silence linger for a bit longer because the silence is actually serving as a conductor that will move the group forward in a way that serves it.

As a facilitator, you will want to consider what kind of relationship you currently have with silence, how you see the value of silence, and how you might respond to silence as you lead affinity groups.

- Are you comfortable with silence, or does it cause you discomfort?
- In your opinion, what is the value of silence?
- How might you respond to silence as you facilitate affinity groups?

- What physical cues does your body offer you to let you know the silence in a group is generative and transformative versus connected to stagnant energy in a group?

Structure and Spaciousness

My dear friend Kerri Kelly, an activist, yoga teacher, and practitioner—and a rabble-rouser—talks about the balance of structure and space in her work. Often, when she speaks about the balance of structure and space, she compares a yoga posture to whatever is happening in the facilitation or meeting we are co-leading. In yoga asana, the poses and movement based part of the practice of yoga, as people move through different poses and make different shapes with their bodies, it is important to provide structure. This might look like offering physical cues for someone to move their arm or leg in a particular direction. It could be letting people know how long they will hold a posture or reminding them the breath can support them in settling into the posture. In yoga asana, structure also relates to the design of a sequence and how poses link together, or to how the practice opens and closes. As people explore different physical postures, they also need space to move into the posture, adjust as needed, notice how the posture feels, and adjust again if needed. They need space to explore the structure they've created with their bodies.

The process I just described is an excellent analogy for what we as facilitators need to provide. As facilitators, we need to provide enough structure by presenting content about topics such as the Ladder of Empowerment for People of Color, the self-system, racial hierarchy, and internalized racial oppression, and we need to give affinity groups space to explore how these different things affect them. We need to give groups space to adjust our plan or continue to explore something that enlivens them at the moment. We need to give groups the space to reflect and the space to co-create the group with us. As a facilitator, you either already know or will learn when something needs more time. You will learn how much content to present and how much structure to provide and when to let go and allow the group to move in the direction it desires. You will learn to trust yourself and to trust that you know what is needed. And you will learn to have the wisdom to ask the group what they need. In general, I think about how I want to open and close a space. If I am sharing content, which I typically am in an affinity group, I consider how much time I want to spend on content and what concept I would like to cover during the affinity group. I always want there to be time for reflection in an affinity group, either or both large- and small-group discussions, or time for discussion in the large group.

- As a facilitator, are you more comfortable with structure or space?
- How do you imagine balancing the two based on what the group needs?
- How might you respond to someone who would like more structure when you believe what is needed is space?
- How would you describe how you will use structure and space for the affinity group you are facilitating?

An Understanding of Intersectionality

Intersectionality is a lens through which you can see where power comes and collides, where it interlocks and intersects.

—KIMBERLÉ CRENSHAW, "Kimberlé Crenshaw on Intersectionality, More Than Two Decades Later," Columbia Law (website)

In the "Shared Language" section of chapter 1, I offered Kimberlé Crenshaw's definition of intersectionality as an analytical framework for understanding how aspects of a person's social and political identities combine to create different modes of discrimination and privilege. As mentioned in chapter 5, as a facilitator of an affinity group for People of Color you need to understand that people are bringing their whole selves, not just their racial identity but all of their embodied identities, into the affinity group. While your focus will be on racial identity in a BIPOC affinity group, it's important to have a framework to better understand how other identities—sexual orientation, religion, gender identity and expression, ability, citizenship, and others—intersect with a person's racial identity.

For example, when I have been in a group with cisgender women and men and nonbinary and trans BIPOC people, it has been essential for me to understand and expect that sexism, heterosexism, and transphobia might affect the group dynamic. In groups like this, cisgender men might feel like they can take up more space because of their indoctrination in a patriarchal society. I have held BIPOC affinity groups where I have had to remind the group to use the proper pronouns for someone in the group who identified as nonbinary or trans (or both) and used they/them pronouns. I have also encountered groups that lack nuance and cannot focus on race while also remembering how all systems of oppression are intertwined. You can set the tone for the affinity group by letting the participants know the focus will be on race, and you can also share your understanding of intersectionality at the beginning of the group. In addition, you can create some community-care practices or agreements, like the ones listed in chapter 5, that support the people in the group to allow them to feel as if they can not only talk about their racial identity but also bring their whole selves into the group.

- As a facilitator why is it important for you to have a deep understanding of intersectionality?
- What intersectional identities do you embody?
- As you facilitate, what might it look like for you to acknowledge that you will focus on race in the affinity group while also encouraging group participants to remember that they and other group participants are having an intersectional experience in the affinity group and world?

The Ability to Navigate Conflict

In large part, dominant culture has conditioned us to be conflict avoidant. It has conditioned us to uphold a culture of politeness when the white supremacy culture has been anything but polite to us. Even though I was conditioned to keep the peace if possible, my mother taught me that sometimes creating peace is only possible once we talk through the things that we need to talk through. I am not afraid of conflict, and when I am facilitating and conflict arises, navigating it promotes growth and development of my facilitation skills. Addressing and navigating conflict can also create the potential for growth in the group.

Whenever people come together, even people who have a shared experience of systemic racism, conflict can arise. In my time facilitating BIPOC affinity groups, I have not experienced knockdown, drag-out conflicts, but I have experienced conflicts based on misunderstanding or limited perspectives. There are many conflict resolution skills you can employ as a facilitator, and all of the skills just discussed—self-awareness, patience, compassion, listening, silence, the balance of structure and spaciousness, and an understanding of intersectionality—come into play when we are navigating a conflict.

As you facilitate affinity groups for People of Color, look for what might be under the surface, and if you find something that needs to be exposed so that the group can move forward, bring it to the surface. As you do this, consider whether or not a conflict needs to be resolved in the large affinity group or in a smaller group or space. Consider whether a simple pause or break will allow the conflict to resolve. If you are working in a community or an organization, you might have some insider information about possible conversational land mines and pain points within a group, and you might be able to anticipate what or who might cause a conflict. If you do have this information, you can keep this in mind as you offer or co-create community-care practices or agreements within the group.

Last, consider how you will respond if someone in the group calls on someone, or calls someone else in or out.[2] Each one of these is a distinct practice and can cause someone to become defensive or to be a space of gratitude because someone cared enough about them to call them in or up. Later in this chapter I share some about self-care as a facilitator, and it feels important to mention here that engaging in a grounding practice like breathing, journaling, meditating, or something else that grounds you will support you as you facilitate, in particular when conflict arises in the group.

- What is your relationship with conflict?
- How do you typically respond when conflict arises while you are facilitating or co-facilitating?
- Why is conflict healthy for a group process?

Throw Out the Agenda

The final skill on my list of essential facilitator skills is to know when to throw out the agenda. Dominant culture has taught many of us to be wedded to an agenda, which in my experience can put pressure on me to follow a plan, even though unexpected things may arise while I am facilitating. Having an agenda can be helpful, but being wedded to it can limit our ability to facilitate what is needed by the group. I encourage you to create whatever plan and agenda you might need for your affinity group but also to be willing to move in a way that may seem off-course but is actually guiding the group to exactly where they need to be. The most potent affinity groups I have experienced as either a participant or a leader have been when I or the person facilitating the space has been willing to be flexible and shape-shift as needed in response to what the group was calling or asking for.

- How comfortable do you feel about creating an agenda and then moving away from it to meet the needs of the group?
- What would support you in deepening your practice of flexibility as you facilitate?

These are some of the most important skills I believe one has to embody if one is going to facilitate a BIPOC affinity group or, really, any group. There may be other skills you bring to facilitation that have supported you in growing into a more effective facilitator. I want to give you an opportunity to reflect on these skills:

- In addition to the skills just listed, what other skills feel important to you as a facilitator of a BIPOC group to embody?
- What are your strengths as a facilitator?
- What are your growing edges as a facilitator?

SELF-CARE FOR THE FACILITATOR

I conclude this chapter by offering information about self-care for a facilitator. I could have included self-care on the list of important skills for a BIPOC affinity group facilitator to embody. I didn't because many of us are in a practice of trying to figure out what self-care means to us. Many of us are in the process of trying to realize the importance of self-care and contemplating how self-care and collective care are interconnected. This is a growing edge for many of us. As BIPOC people, we live in a white supremacy culture that has no interest in our being cared for, so we must find ways to care for ourselves, not necessarily as an act of resistance against white supremacy but because we deserve care and being cared for. There is an entire history of our caretaking white-bodied people; if we want to thrive, we must prioritize our own care and the care of other BIPOC people.

I believe that self-care is connected to our ability to sustain ourselves and thrive. If I do not care for myself, I will not be resourced spiritually, physically, emotionally, financially, and mentally. When I am not adequately resourced, I find it difficult for me to resource others. Our cups must be full to lead BIPOC affinity groups. If our cups are empty, we will further deplete ourselves in a white supremacy culture that wants us to feel empty and exhausted all of the time. My self-care practice looks like prayer, meditation, movement, laughter, sharing space in affinity groups with other Black and Indigenous POC, cooking, taking a pause when needed, resting and sitting in a circle with comrades with the sole purpose of being with one another, not working, and just being. All of these things allow me to feel resourced and centered, which I most definitely need to feel as I lead groups.

REFLECTION QUESTIONS

- What does your self-care practice look like?
- What would you like your self-care practice to look like?
- Why is self-care important to a BIPOC person?
- Why is self-care important to a facilitator of BIPOC affinity groups?
- How is your practice of self-care connected to the care of other BIPOC people?

These reflection questions are not meant to make you feel shame if you are finding it difficult to care for yourself at this time. They are meant to invite you to consider the practice of self-care a critical practice for your sustenance, survival, and ability to thrive. Revisit the reflection questions as you wish, and my wish for you is that you and we are cared for and that we have all the room and space we need to care for ourselves.

"Everything is being disrupted right now. The only solution is for us to actually start asking, okay, how do we care for ourselves?"

—LAMA ROD OWENS, *Finding Refuge* podcast, November 18, 2021

CHAPTER 7

USE YOUR MAGIC

Don't be afraid of your magic—use it.

—ADRIENNE MAREE BROWN, *Holding Change:*
The Way of Emergent Strategy Facilitation and Mediation

I FIND THINGS ALL THE TIME! Four-leaf clovers, heart-shaped biscuits, heart-shaped clouds—so many hearts—love letters, sand dollars miles from the nearest beach, and more. I receive all of the things I find as signs from the universe because I do believe the universe is in constant communication with us—all of us. One day, while walking in the woods, I found a large wooden spoon. It looked handmade, and it was beautiful. I found it, or rather it found me, during a time when the universe, my ancestors, and Spirit were facilitating significant change in my life.

I was preparing to move across the country, going through a separation that would lead to an eventual divorce, leaving a full-time career as a clinical social worker, writing my first book, *Skill in Action: Radicalizing Your Yoga Practice to Create a Just World*, and leaving a community of which I had been part for over twenty years. Upon finding the spoon, I knew that the universe was communicating with me about my magic. An image of a cauldron and people gathered around it stirring and adding ingredients to the cauldron came into my mind as I picked up the spoon. I didn't know what role this wooden spoon would play in my life, but it was packed up in a box when I moved across the country to Portland, Oregon, in June 2017 and then again in June 2018 when I moved back across the country, returning home to North Carolina.

Later, in March 2021, I was co-leading a training about how to facilitate artfully and skillfully. We asked participants to bring in an object representative of their connection with facilitation. As a leader of the training, I also brought in an object, the wooden spoon I had found on my walk in the woods years earlier. When it was my time to introduce myself to the group I was co-leading, I shared my wooden spoon to represent how it feels when I facilitate a group process. I shared that when I facilitate, I feel like I am holding that wooden spoon, stirring the pot, adding ingredients and weaving a spell. If I or someone in the group adds an ingredient that shifts the group's focus, causes harm or disengagement to our metaphorical cauldron, our spell may have to take a different direction than we foresaw. This is not always a negative experience. We need various spells for different occasions. If I or someone in the group adds an ingredient that supports connection, the release of what we are holding that isn't ours, self-inquiry, deeper connection with the heart, courage, vulnerability, accountability and grace, everyone might feel the magic of our spell in the air. This chapter explores what ingredients we need in order to generate conversation, move, slow down, set boundaries, or pause a group. It offers various facilitator techniques and strategies that will support you in becoming a better facilitator.

GENERATING DISCUSSION

In chapter 6, I spoke about the use of silence in your facilitation. There are times when silence is precisely what the group needs, and there are times when someone needs to start the conversation to get the group into a dialogue or discussion. I imagine you've had the experience of a facilitator offering a prompt to the group and then waiting, waiting, and waiting some more for someone to be the first person to respond to the prompt. You may have also had the experience as a facilitator or in a group process where someone starts the dialogue and a few people share. Then a few more people want to share, and time runs out for everyone who decides they want to share to have space to speak. In my experience of facilitating BIPOC affinity groups, it doesn't take long for the group to dive into a discussion. Often we are so grateful to be in space with each other, and this gratitude comes out in the form of folks chatting away with one another.

In the event that the group is particularly quiet, here are some prompts and techniques you can use to get people talking.

Journaling

Some prompts you might offer if you are inviting group participants to journal at the beginning of the affinity group or after the opening meditation or centering are:

- How do you feel?
- What physical sensations do you notice?
- What emotions are moving through?
- What do you know now?
- What question is present for you?
- How does it feel to be in a BIPOC affinity space?

After participants have journaled, invite everyone to do a go-around and share one sentence from their reflection.

Go-Around

If you want to check in with everyone and do not wish to invite group participants to journal and share, you can ask the following prompts and encourage each person to share by either going around the circle or speaking as they feel moved to . . .

- Share a feeling.
- Share a color that represents how you are feeling right now.
- Share a weather report—use terms a meteorologist would use to describe how you feel. For example, cloudy with a hint of sun, overcast, sunny and bright, etc.
- Call the name of an ancestor into the space—living or deceased—a human, a teaching, an animal or pet, something from the natural world, or something else that inspires.
- Share something you feel grateful for as a result of being in an affinity group.

Pair Shares or Small-Group Shares

It is routine for me to invite people into dyads or smaller groups to share with one another. This technique is useful because sometimes people do not want to talk in a large group, and smaller groups can create conditions that make space for everyone to share if they would like. Dyads and small groups are a more intimate setting for someone to share vulnerably with someone else, particularly about experiences of racism, socialization, conditioning, racial trauma, etc. In addition to providing a more intimate setting, small groups or dyads can be useful when time doesn't allow for everyone to share in the main space.

PRACTICES TO MAKE SURE FOLKS HAVE
THE SPACE THEY NEED TO SHARE

We have all been deeply socialized about when to communicate, how much space to take up, and who should be able to take up space. For example, our patriarchal culture conditions people socialized as men to take up space and talk while it conditions people socialized as women to be quiet and not take up as much space. Our ableist culture conditions those of us who are physically abled to feel entitled to space while it conditions people who are physically disabled to stay quiet. As mentioned in previous chapters, our intersectional identities influence how we show up in groups and create group dynamics that could get in the way of everyone feeling as if they have room and space to share.

Many of us as BIPOC people have been conditioned to stay quiet while white-bodied people take up all of the space. White supremacy rewards white-bodied people for taking up space and reinforces the belief that white-bodied people deserve the floor at all times. The eagerness about having a space to share freely with other BIPOC people without white-bodied people present or shutting down a conversation because of their discomfort can translate into someone talking a lot simply because they finally have the opportunity to share about their experience with other BIPOC people. This can create a dynamic in the group where people's eagerness gets in the way of everyone being able to share. It is your job as the leader of the affinity group to ensure that everyone has the space to share. Here are some techniques I routinely use to make sure everyone does have the space to talk and share.

RELY ON THE COMMUNITY-CARE PRACTICES At the point in the affinity group when I explain community-care practices, I mention something about wanting to create a space where everyone has time to share. By doing this I am setting an expectation that we need to work together as a group to ensure everyone has the room they need to share. I also tell the group that if someone has shared twice and there are people in the group who haven't shared at all, I will ask the person who has shared twice to wait to share again to give space to others. This is an excellent time to invite participants to practice discernment about when and what they share.

USE A TALKING OBJECT Throughout history and even today, many Indigenous communities have used a talking stick or object to manage communication and to create a culture of respect in groups and circles. If you are meeting with your affinity group in person, you can bring in a stick, rock, feather, or anything that can easily be held by the person who has the floor and passed on to others in the group when it is their turn to share. Only the person holding the object is able to talk. If you want to use a talking object as you are doing a go-around to check in with everyone, you will ask who would like to share first, give them the talking stick, and then move around the circle. If a person receives the talking object and isn't ready to share, they can pass it on to the next person, and the group can come back to them when they feel ready. Using a talking object aids in decreasing side conversations because an expectation is set that the only person who can talk is the person with the talking object.

TIME-LIMITED SHARING In general, I do not like to shut down a conversation when someone speaks too long. The use of a timer can support people in deepening their understanding of how much space they take up, help them clarify the most important things to share with the group, and be in an experience where everyone has the same amount of time for a task, in this case, sharing. Using a timer in particularly large groups can be helpful as well. As the facilitator, you can keep time and let the group know the amount of time they will have to share. If they don't fill the full amount of time allotted, I move on to the next group participant. If they are in the middle of a sentence when the timer goes off, people can finish their thought or sentence so as to not cut them off midsentence. You could also assign this time-keeping role to one of the group participants.

ASKING DIRECTLY If you notice that someone hasn't shared in the group, you can directly ask them if they would like to share. You might say, "Patrice, we haven't heard from you yet. Would you like to share?" If Patrice doesn't want to share, that is just fine, and you will have given Patrice an opportunity to share if they would like to.

BOUNDARIES I have found that some people want to use their time in an affinity group as a therapy session. I am a trained therapist, but when I lead affinity groups, I am not leading a group therapy process unless I am leading an affinity group in a therapeutic setting for clients of color. As BIPOC people, we experience racialized trauma, and affinity groups are one space where we can begin to heal this trauma. While affinity spaces are a place to process and heal our racialized trauma, they are not mental health support groups. As a facilitator, you do not want to be in the position of holding space as a therapist would, and you do not want the group to have to hold someone else's trauma that might be better processed with a therapist or counselor. I want to acknowledge the lack of culturally specific mental health resources available to us and be clear that your role as an affinity group facilitator is to facilitate, not provide therapy.

White supremacy and racism cause physical, emotional, mental, and spiritual trauma, and we lack spaces where we can process our trauma. Some of us do not know how much trauma we are carrying until we are afforded a space to process. We might be so glad to be seen, witnessed, and supported that we don't realize we are asking the group to hold trauma or suggest therapeutic support in ways that are outside the purview of an affinity group. Because of this dynamic, you may need to set a boundary with a group participant who is seeking something from the space that the affinity process isn't designed for. If you notice someone sharing a lot with the group, and sharing things that call for more therapeutic support, you can gently interrupt the person, remind the group of the community-care practices, and let them know you want to make sure there is space for everyone to share and be heard. Setting boundaries can be a difficult, but it is a very important practice.

Boundaries aren't bad; they're necessary. When you set a boundary, you are modeling to the group how to share airspace and time in a group. You are calling attention to ways an individual's actions might impact an entire group, and you are inviting the group to be discerning about what and how much they share. There are compassionate ways of setting boundaries. You do not want to shame or blame the person who is taking up too much space because they need something bigger than what the affinity group can offer.

When I set a boundary because someone needs more than the group can offer, often I first set the boundary in the large group, and at a later time I check in with the individual group participant. Often they may have been unaware of how much space they were taking up or they are in need of something in addition to the support an affinity group can provide. I check in with them and share what I noticed and ask if they have additional support, such as a counselor or therapist. If they are interested in starting therapy, I offer them a list of recommendations. If you do not have a list of local therapists or mental health support systems, you can reach out to a mental health center or college counseling center to ask for recommendations. In addition, many people search psychologytoday.com for therapists and mental health support.

RESPONDING TO HARM AND CREATING CONDITIONS FOR REPAIR For the most part, the community-care practices will support you and the group in creating an environment where less harm occurs. They are the guideposts for the group. Even so, harm could happen in the group, and having some strategies to respond to it is helpful. In affinity groups I have led, harm often occurs when someone's experience is negated. For example, when a person of Asian descent assumes their experience is exactly the same as a Black person's. We know that every BIPOC person experiences systemic racism; the effects of anti-Blackness and the racial hierarchy mean that Black people have a very different experience of racism than a person of Asian descent. Of course, this is also context specific. As mentioned in chapter 4, when COVID-19 emerged, government leaders across the globe began to directly and indirectly encourage hate crimes, racism, or xenophobia by using anti-Chinese rhetoric. COVID-19 shifted the context and, though we know that the context influences our experience as People of Color, it is still important to hold the nuance presented because of living within a culture that subscribes to a racial hierarchy.

Harm occurs when people misgender folks in the group. It happens when someone interrupts someone else to counter the point they are making. Sharing different perspectives is important, and when people cut each other off, it feels harmful and can shut down the conversation. Harm arises when we cannot hold the complexities we all bring into spaces and the nuanced experiences we have.

When harm occurs, I use different strategies to respond to it. I remind people of the community-care practices. I name patterns, like the pattern of misgendering people because of how we have been socialized to think about gender as binary and easily discernible based on appearances. Or the pattern of someone negating someone else's experience by generalizing their experience onto the entire group. I name when I sense discomfort in the space, and I name when I feel as if the discomfort is a response to something harmful that occurred. I invite the group to remember how nuanced everything we are moving through really is. If someone repeatedly causes harm and has disrupted the group, I might ask that person to leave, or I might pause the group and have a private conversation with the person who caused the harm outside of the full group. We cannot bypass harm, and even as we work to create safer conditions than the conditions dominant culture has created for us, spaces can become unsafe very quickly.

Creating conditions for repair is complicated because everyone might need something different, and there are some best practices that speak to how we can begin to repair or recover after harm has occurred.

PROTOCOL FOR RESPONDING AFTER HARM HAS OCCURRED

1. Take a deep breath.
2. Acknowledge the harm.
3. Attend to the person who has been harmed and ask if they need anything or what is needed.
4. Without rushing to fix or save people, ask the person who caused the harm to apologize.
5. If the person who has been harmed is unsure of what they need, give them time to think about it.
6. If a conversation outside of the affinity group between the person who caused the harm and the person who was harmed is needed, make space for this to happen. You might offer to mediate the conversation unless there is someone more appropriate to fill this role.

Take some time to consider how you might respond to harm. You might explore the following prompts to support you in this reflection process:

- Are there experiences when harm has occurred in a group you were participating in and the facilitator effectively responded to it and worked to create conditions for healing and repair?
- How might community-care practices support you as you respond to harm?
- What strategies and tools have you used to name the harm when it has occurred and to lead the group into a process of healing?

One more type of harm could occur in your affinity group—a white-bodied person could come into the space. In over twenty years of facilitating affinity groups, this has only happened to me twice. I find that if I'm working with a white-bodied co-facilitator as part of a biracial training team and if we have set up affinity groups appropriately, most white-bodied people know not to come into the BIPOC affinity space.

In one of the settings, I was offering a community anti-racism workshop and we split into affinity groups. A white woman came to the BIPOC affinity group, and I didn't know she was white. I try not to make assumptions about people's racial identities because I have known several people who appear white-bodied who are, in fact, not white but are able to pass as white or Black. Once the affinity group began, the white woman shared that she was white and that her racialized experience felt more like the experience of a person of color. There is no way that she could fully understand what it is like for us to navigate a white supremacy culture, but she thought she could. After she shared, I checked in with the people in the affinity group so they could share about the impact of the white woman's actions on them, and I asked her to leave. She was quite resistant but eventually left our space, and we processed what had just happened and moved on with our affinity group.

The other time a white person came into an affinity group was in the context of an organization. We were facilitating a two-day racial equity training for a large organization. We split into affinity groups. I was co-leading my group with another Black facilitator, and a white woman came into that group. This situation was a bit trickier than the previously described scenario. This white woman didn't want to leave. Needless to say, her behavior disrupted the group and impacted the participants deeply. Her entitlement was gross and sucked the air out of the room. She believed she could be wherever she wanted to be and do whatever she wanted to do. This was amplified by the fact that we were in an organization where she held more power than some of the BIPOC people in the affinity group. Her actions most certainly showed us how she misused her power. We had to ask the white facilitators to come into our space to get the white woman to leave. After the affinity group was over, we spoke with the directors of the organization and suggested a restorative justice process where the white woman could account for her actions and work to change her behavior. We also offered extra support to the BIPOC affinity group by facilitating three additional affinity groups.

We know that white-bodied individuals have been socialized to be-lieve they are entitled to the moon, sun, stars, and really anything they want. This socialization leads to the egregious behavior I described. It is likely you will not encounter a white-bodied individual coming into your BIPOC affinity space; still, take some time to consider what you will do if it does happen.

PRACTICE TO CREATE DEEPER UNDERSTANDING

People who attend your BIPOC affinity group will have stories to share about their experiences. They may be aware of their conscious responses to racialized trauma and internalized racism and may also lack such awareness of their unconscious responses to racialized trauma and inter-nalized racism. Part of the practice that occurs in BIPOC affinity groups is consciousness-raising and supporting participants in deepening their understanding of how racism and white supremacy have affected them. Earlier in this book I shared some content centered on the Ladder of Empowerment for People of Color, the self-system, and internalized racial oppression, material that you can use to deepen understanding. There are some strategies you can employ to further raise consciousness as you facilitate BIPOC affinity groups.

Educational Tools

You can ask participants to read an article, watch a movie, or listen to a podcast prior to participating in an affinity group. These types of re-sources can spark conversation and support affinity group participants in developing deeper insight into how living in a white supremacy culture has affected them.

Quotes

I have included several quotes in this book. This is not only to enhance the text and bring in different voices of color but also to raise conscious-ness. At times, to aid me as I facilitate, I have chosen to print out quotes from several different People of Color and post them on the wall. This can be helpful for people because the quotes can be a focal point for someone who is seeking inspiration, a sense of groundedness, or connec-tion. It can also generate discussion and surface different perspectives. Another way to use quotes is to invite group participants to choose a quote that most resonates with them and to share with the group why the quote resonates.

Ancestral Trauma and Post-Traumatic Growth

You can provide a mini-lecture or discussion about intergenerational trauma, defining it and asking group participants to consider how they carry the trauma of their ancestors in their bones. If you are going to move through an activity like this and lead a discussion about intergenerational trauma, it is important to also bring awareness and attention to intergenerational resilience and post-traumatic growth. Post-traumatic growth, a theory developed by psychologists Richard Tedeschi and Lawrence Calhoun in the mid-1990s, is when someone has found a way to make meaning out of their experience of trauma in order to live their life in a different way than they did prior to experiencing trauma. White supremacy is ongoing, and therefore our exposure to the trauma it breeds is ongoing. Even so, in our bones and blood we have memories of our ancestors making meaning of their lives and thriving so we could be here now.

It is important to bring people's awareness to this fact and to focus on both the trauma and what manifests from it and also on the ways we as BIPOC people have been able to grow, thrive, and create spaces for ourselves where we experience liberation and moments of transcendence of the confines of white supremacy.

An example of this for me is my great-grandmother, Angie. Even though her parents were enslaved and she was born into enslavement, this isn't the only part of her lived experience that lives inside me. Angie was feisty, strong, smart, creative, vibrant, and sassy. She found a way to take care of her family after her husband died of tuberculosis, and even though she worked as a domestic worker for most of her life, she was joyful. She loved her children, grandchildren, and great-grandchildren. She was always talking to us about how proud she was of us. Despite all of the trauma she experienced because of a system that enslaved people like her and attempted to strip away their humanity, she lived her life in a way that wasn't defined by the limitations white supremacy placed onto her. While I move with Angie in my blood, I embody both her trauma, the ways she found to heal from white supremacy and the patriarchy, and her strength and resilience.

One ritual I ask participants to move through is to think of a mentor, ancestor, or teacher who inspired them and reminded them of who they really are. Once participants have thought of this person, I ask them to speak the name of this individual and to bring their energy and resilience into the group. Sometimes they tell a short story about the individual.

Fishbowl

In an affinity group, a fishbowl is exactly what it sounds like, an opportunity for one person or a small group of people to be witnessed by a larger group of people. The purpose of fishbowls is to allow for an opportunity to dive more deeply into a situation someone may need guidance around. Fishbowls can be used to raise awareness or deepen understanding and to allow someone or a small group to deepen insight into an issue they are moving through. If you want to set up a fishbowl, you can invite one person or a few people to sit in a row or circle of chairs, and the rest of the group will observe the process. You might invite a few people if you are in the context of an organization or community and there is a small group trying to problem-solve or heal from a particular incident that has occurred. The prompt you offer to the group can be something related to what they want to develop, or to facilitate a deeper understanding of an issue they need support with. You can begin by asking the fishbowl participants to share some of what they need support around or want to understand better. Give them a few minutes to share. After they have shared, the group who is observing can ask open-ended questions such as the following:

- How do you feel in your body as you talk about this?
- As you think about this event, what color do you associate with the experience?
- What do you wish had happened versus what did happen?
- What do you need?
- What do you want us to know?
- How does it feel to be witnessed?
- What insight did you gain from the experience?
- What other perspectives could be important for you to be aware of?

The person in the fishbowl can choose to answer these questions, and often deeper insight is gained from this experience.

As we know, there are many responses one can have after experiencing overt racism or living in a racist culture, including but not limited to trauma, tenderness, grief, anger, rage, sadness, confusion, apathy, and depression. Most often we need a reparative process to occur after having experienced racism, but many times, this isn't afforded to us. A fishbowl can be used to emulate a reparative process and cultivate healing. I have seen a fishbowl facilitated where a person of color has shared about a time when they experienced racism. After they have shared, people observing the fishbowl ask open-ended questions. The person can choose to answer the questions or not. To conclude this kind of fishbowl, you can invite everyone in the space to respond to the following question: What did (fill in the name of the person) in the fishbowl need instead of what happened? What did they need to hear, experience, remember, etc.?

I was once co-leading a training in which we explored a fishbowl activity in a racially mixed group. A Black woman shared about an experience of leading a training herself where a white participant shared about ancestry in a harmful way that left the Black woman leading the training feeling traumatized and as if she had to caretake the white woman. She shared this experience with us, and one of the facilitators holding the space with me asked the group to share what should have happened and what support the Black woman should have received during her training. It was beautiful to witness people affirm the Black woman, and I could feel some of the residual trauma from the experience she shared with us being released and let go, making way for healing. White supremacy isn't going to engage in the process of repair, but we can create conditions of repair for ourselves by affirming each other and countering whatever it is any one of us may have internalized as a result of how white supremacy and racism operate.

Body-Centered Practices

I believe we carry everything in our bodies and that our bodies remember everything we've ever experienced, even when we cannot consciously remember. The body is something we are born into, and it weathers so much—both the joys of life and the traumas and tragedies. As many people have said before, the body remembers. The body records. The body processes. The body holds and releases. We have experienced traumas that have moved us away from our bodies. People of color, and members of any group who experiences marginalization, have to navigate systems that would much rather our bodies not be in existence, and still, somehow, our bodies are here. By engaging in practices to come back into awareness of our bodies, we reclaim our wholeness and humanity as we heal the wounds inflicted upon us by white supremacy.

You do not have to be a yoga teacher or movement specialist to bring awareness to the body. I believe body awareness is innate to us and that we experience individual and cultural traumas due to familial dysfunction, trauma being passed on intergenerationally, and systems of oppression that move us from our innate ability to remember we inhabit divine vessels that we call bodies. There are several ways to bring awareness to the body and invite affinity group participants to deepen their relationship with their bodies. I will list a few below and encourage you to add to this list.

Deep Breaths

In chapter 5, I shared the importance of beginning an affinity group with an opening centering. You might open your affinity group by asking the group to take a few deep breaths. Countless studies have been conducted on the nervous system effect of taking a deep breath. The data from studies about the breath and engaging the breath to shift the way one feels at any given moment overwhelmingly suggests that taking a deep breath stimulates the vagus nerve, which comprises the main nerves of your parasympathetic nervous system. When the vagus nerve activates the parasympathetic nervous system it is an indication to the body and mind that it is time to relax and de-stress. This process seems critical if we want to downregulate, recenter ourselves, and heal from racialized trauma in the face of all that we have been subjected to because of systems of dominance such as white supremacy. Lead a few rounds of deep breathing. You will notice an energy shift in the room. You might even ask the group to share about their experience and provide some education about the vagus nerve and body-centered practices that stimulate this nerve.

Body Scan

A body scan is a tool to elicit deep relaxation and increase awareness of the body. You can use the script that follows as is or adapt it to lead a body scan.

SCRIPT FOR THREE-MINUTE BODY SCAN For this practice, you can sit in a chair or on the earth, or lie down on the floor. You can close your eyes, soften your gaze, or find a grounding focal point for this practice.

Begin by bringing your attention and awareness into your body.

Take a moment to notice your body seated or lying on the earth, and feel the weight of your body on the chair or on the floor.

Take a few deep breaths.

As you take a deep breath, invite in energy, and as you exhale, feel yourself relax more deeply.

I invite you to notice your feet, the sensations of your feet touching the floor.

Now I invite you to notice your legs against the chair or the floor.

Notice your back against the chair or floor.

Bring your attention to your stomach area. If your stomach is tense or tight, see if you can let it soften. Take a deep breath.

Notice your hands. Are your hands tense or tight? See if you can allow them to soften.

Notice your arms. Feel any sensation in your arms. Let your shoulders be soft.

Notice your neck and throat. Let them be soft. Relax.

Soften your jaw. Let your face and facial muscles be soft.

Then notice your whole body present. Take one more breath.

Be aware of your whole body as best you can. Take a deep breath. And then, when you're ready, gently blink open your eyes or lift your gaze and take a few deep breaths.

Shaking

Those of you who have furry friends in your life may have noticed that when they experience something traumatic, they tend to shake right afterward. They do this to shake off what happened and to activate the parasympathetic nervous system, which signals to their brain that it is time to calm down and relax. We, too, can activate our parasympathetic nervous system in the same way. By shaking. This practice might be useful after a tense conversation or a share that may have reactivated trauma for someone or many people in the affinity group. To lead a shaking practice or meditation, explain the purpose of shaking and how it activates the parasympathetic nervous system after a traumatic event has occurred.

Often this practice can feel most impactful if one is standing up, but people can practice this exercise while seated. Invite group participants to stand or sit. If they choose to stand, invite them to stand with their feet hip distance apart, soften their knees, and relax their shoulders. Then invite them to gently bounce, sway side to side, lift and lower their shoulders, and shake out their hands and feet. They can even shake their hips too. Ask them to try to shake the entire body. You might even decide to play music as they are moving through the practice. Allow the group to shake for anywhere from five to ten minutes. If this feels too long for your group, you can invite the group to shake for two minutes. If may be new or feel like an unusual way to move the body, so it can take some time for folks to get into this kind of practice. Allowing enough time for them to get into the practice is important. After the group has completed the shaking meditation, invite them to take some deep breaths and to notice how they feel. You might even open the space for people to share about the experience.

Please feel free to add other body-centered practices to this list.

APPLICATION

In this section I invite you to consider different scenarios you could encounter as you facilitate and how you might respond using some of the suggested facilitator techniques presented in this chapter.

Scenario A

In a racially mixed anti-racism or racial equity training, you and your white-bodied co-trainer explain the role of affinity groups in preparation to move into them. After you both offer your explanations, a white-bodied person reacts negatively to the group being split into affinity groups based on race. As best they can, your white-bodied co-trainer addresses the white-bodied person who disrupted the entire group with their behavior, and you all proceed to move into affinity groups. When you meet with your BIPOC affinity group, people are angry, upset, and frustrated. Some group participants share how tired they are of white people taking up so much space and feeling entitled to having things go exactly as they would like. There is tension in the group.

- Since this has occurred at the start of the affinity group, how might you respond to create a positive opening for the group?
- What facilitator techniques might you use to shift the energy in the group and respond to the different emotions participants are expressing?

Scenario B

You have completed the opening check-in with your affinity group. You have opened the space for folks to share as they feel moved to and someone has shared twice and is about to share a third time. The other times they shared, they shared a lot of information, and you can tell that what they shared felt like a lot for the group to hold and respond to.

- How might you set a boundary with this group participant?
- What guidelines might you remind the group members of to encourage them to be aware of how much space they individually might be taking up?
- Would you intervene in the large group or ask the group to take a pause and then take the person aside and speak with them?
- If you are feeling activated in response to the person sharing so much and seeming to be unaware of how much space they are taking up, how might you center yourself so you can continue to facilitate the affinity group?

Scenario C

You are facilitating a BIPOC affinity group, not a group broken down by ethnicity or individual racial identities. You have people from various backgrounds and of different ethnicities and races in the group. You have asked the group participants to introduce themselves to the group by sharing their names, pronouns, a land acknowledgment, and how they are feeling at the present moment. You model this by sharing your name, pronouns, a land acknowledgment, and a feeling. A participant introduces themselves with their name, Ara, offers a land acknowledgment, and feeling. During Ara's introduction, Ara shares that Ara is Two-Spirit and that Ara does not use pronouns. Ara asks to be called by Ara's name instead of being referred to using pronouns. After group introductions, you open up discussion. Each time Ara shares Ara's experience of the intersectional

identities Ara embodies, an older Black cisgender man in the group interrupts Ara and says that the affinity group is focused on race, not gender
identity. He speaks at length.

- How might you respond to this?
- What community-care practices would you remind the group of?
- How would you address the harm caused by the Black cisgender
  man and how would you offer care to Ara, the group participant
  who identifies as Two-Spirit?
- If you identify as Two-Spirit, nonbinary, gender nonconforming,
  or transgender, and feel activated by the behavior of the Black
  cisgender man, how would you care for yourself?
- Are there any body-centered practices you would choose to lead to
  release any tension that might be present in the space due to the
  harm that occurred?

These are just a few scenarios that might present themselves as you facilitate affinity groups. These scenarios are not meant to make you nervous
or for you to feel as if you cannot lead a BIPOC affinity group. They are
to support you in thinking about how you can respond to situations that
might arise as you facilitate. Facilitation isn't about perfection; it is about
bringing our own magic into a space and trusting that it will support us as
we facilitate. Facilitating is about the wooden spoon, cauldron, and mix-
ing the ingredients to support the group while also knowing that we may
need to rework our mix or start our spell over again, course-correcting
as we go along.

CHAPTER 8

FACILITATING AFFINITY GROUPS
IN ORGANIZATIONS AND COMMUNITIES

I guess the challenge has always been for me, the most interesting
challenge is, how do we take a constraint and turn it into an opportunity
to make something really unique in the world.

—MEEJIN YOON, in conversation
with the National Endowment for the Arts, 2012

HAVE FACILITATED BIPOC affinity groups within organizations of all sizes, with different missions and visions for their racial justice work. I have facilitated affinity groups in many communities of all sizes that have different hopes and desires for their racial justice work. In communities and organizations alike, people are working within the constraints of an institution and culture that actively creates barriers to block us from experiencing true freedom, barriers based on race and other identities we might embody that are marginalized by dominant culture or are less proximal to power. As communities and organizations seek to make radical change focused on racial equity, unique challenges and opportunities will arise.

Affinity groups in community spaces are expansive. There are options; the sky is the limit. Like we could do this or that. We could do anything. Whereas, when I think about my experience facilitating and participating in organizational affinity groups, we are limited by the confines, the constructs of that institution, or even the particular industry of which the institution is a part. Another dynamic that comes up in communities and organizations is people may not have deep relationships with one another, but building relationship in a

*community feels easier than in an institution because the stakes feel different in
a community. In an institution you have to work alongside the people in your
affinity group every day.*

—STEPHANIE GHOSTON PAUL

In my experience, Stephanie Ghoston Paul is spot-on in her analysis of
the difference in facilitating affinity groups in organizations versus communities. Something else is indeed at stake in communities as opposed to
within organizations. In organizations or institutions, work relationships
can be very different from community relationships because if we meet in
an affinity group in the context of an organization, we have to work with
our coworkers each day. In an affinity group taking place in the community, we do not necessarily have to be in direct and daily communication
or deep relationship with folks who might participate in the group.

Within organizations, our jobs may be at stake if we cannot get along
with our coworkers. We may have deliverables we need to turn in to a superior of color or a white superior. There may be organizational tensions
based on race that are not easily resolvable. We might have taken on work
within an organization to pay the bills, but we may not feel deeply invested
in the racial equity work within the organization for various reasons. Such
reasons might be that, in the past, the organization has tried to take part
in racial equity work and it failed, and we feel traumatized from that experience. We might distrust leadership's intentions and commitment to the
racial equity work and process. This could be for good reasons rooted in
history and our memory of how many organizational leaders have initiated
racial equity processes only to shut them down when things become difficult. Often this kind of shutdown occurs as the culture of the organization
begins to shift and move toward a goal of becoming more racially equitable.
We might feel burned out by the world and the racial inequities and daily
onslaught of white supremacy we are subjected to and simply not have the
energy to put our whole self into the racial equity work our organization
is doing. We might want to keep our heads down and do other work,
even though we are deeply committed to collective liberation for BIPOC
people. We may want a promotion and more positional power so we have
greater agency to make necessary changes that will allow BIPOC people
to feel more supported in the organization. This could translate into our
becoming quiet or not being very vocal about racial inequities within the
institution until we have acquired more positional power.

In communities the situation is different. Generally, we don't owe someone who is part of our community something we said we would deliver on. Other than family, we have more choice in deciding who we are in community versus being placed in roles within an institution where we have no choice but to be in relationship with certain folks. We may choose to actively engage in racial equity work within our community versus having a racial equity process thrust upon us in an organization. Power operates differently in organizations and communities, and communities can rally around a strategy or organizing effort without being faced with the same risks as the ones people face in organizations (such as loss of job, demotion, and work stress).

In addition to these differences between institutions and communities, many organizations interested in becoming anti-racist or more equitable were created according to the ideals and principles of white supremacy and capitalism, such as power hoarding, manifest destiny, more is better, productivity over people, and others. Beliefs and ideals held within communities of color are not inherently rooted in white supremacy and capitalism. White supremacy was designed to split communities of color apart, and many of the ideals held within communities of color are based on interconnectedness and interdependence. Communities of color, and many other groups who experience marginalization because of oppression, often value and practice collectivism, connection, and relationship; we have had to rely on each other and see how we are interconnected to survive.

Organizations may face constraints when setting up BIPOC affinity groups because they have a bottom line, want to measure the results of the equity efforts they are engaged in, and are often under time pressure or pressure to meet a deadline. The entire equity process and the facilitation of affinity groups can be tainted by how white supremacy has become institutionalized within organizations. Some examples of this are a focus on quantitative data, prioritizing productivity over the process and people, centering perfectionism, the belief that there is only one right way to do things, and urgency that is often unfounded and rooted in wanting a quick fix to an issue that has been present for a long time. Racism has been ravaging our lives for centuries. It has been an urgent concern for BIPOC people since race was constructed for sociopolitical reasons and rooted in separation. Organizations often have an intended outcome for their equity process, and this outcome can drive the process more than the people involved in it or the people most impacted by racial inequity.

Organizations and institutions have more formal structures than com-munities. Often, and especially in white-led and for-profit organizations and corporations, these formal structures do not pursue practices that are counter to dominant cultural norms such as valuing connection, collective care, and sharing power. These same structures can be found in nonprofits because they too have institutionalized practices that derive from white supremacy cultural norms. As you facilitate in organizations with formal structures that reinforce white supremacy, know that it might be difficult for members of the affinity group to practice rituals and ways of being that counter dominant cultural norms.

It might take time for people to try new things in the context of an organization because what you are offering them may be very different and outside the organization's current culture. For example, as you know from the centering, opening, breathing, and body-based practices I discussed earlier, I suggest that we give people some time to arrive by breathing deeply and taking a moment to notice what is most present for them as they enter the affinity group. This is counter to dominant cultural norms around how we enter a space, especially in an organization. Usually, peo-ple enter a meeting, and the meeting begins without taking a moment to honor that we have all arrived. There is an agenda that we must follow, and then the meeting is over. Institutions do not often take time to allow for a deep breath or pause. If you suggest these kinds of practices—new kinds of rituals—in organizations, you might experience some resistance to them. There may be more receptivity to them in community affinity groups. (In chapter 10, I share more about why ritual is an essential part of BIPOC affinity groups.)

In addition to considering how opening with a breath or pause might affect an affinity group taking place within an organization, it is essential for you to contemplate how you will support BIPOC people in transitioning back to their workspaces where they might encounter white colleagues or bosses. This is tricky because organizations often set aside sixty to seventy-five minutes for an affinity group to meet each month, and folks come into the affinity group from one meeting and go to the next meeting after the affinity group. BIPOC affinity groups can feel like safer spaces for BIPOC people to process and share about their experiences of being BIPOC in the organization, especially in white-led organizations. BIPOC people can experience a spaciousness in BIPOC affinity groups that is not otherwise present in their day-to-day interactions with white-bodied colleagues or the role they might have within a particular organization.

When we open this affinity space and then send people back into a space that potentially feels constraining to them because of how white supremacy functions within it, it is important to speak to the transition from affinity back into a racially mixed organization. Speak to this reality at the beginning of the affinity group. Let participants know that you will leave time at the end of the affinity group for people to share about what they need as they transition out of the affinity group. If time and your consultant contract allow, you can offer some extra coaching hours to BIPOC people who are participants in the affinity group.

When organizations contact me to work with them to create a more racially equitable organization, most often they think they know exactly what they want, but in actuality they have no idea what they truly need. If an organization is white-led, or a few white leaders contact me, the pattern I notice more often than not is that before I am able to make recommendations about what would make their organization more equitable, the leaders try to tell me their thoughts on this matter even after having called an outside consultant, myself, for help. To me, this feels like a replication of white supremacy and a pattern of whiteness. White-bodied people have been conditioned and socialized to believe they know best, even if they do not know anything about the topic at hand.

If a racially mixed leadership team contacts me, sometimes the People of Color on the team have ideas about what is most needed based on the experience they and other BIPOC people are having within the organization. Sometimes white leaders take the lead from BIPOC people and at other times they get in the way. If a BIPOC-led organization contacts me, it may still have questions about what is needed or how to go about their racial equity work, and it is more likely there is at least some shared understanding of how systemic racism is impacting them individually and as a collective group within their organization.

My approach with organizations is to do an intake assessment, which includes gathering an understanding of the work the organization has done in the past related to racial equity and any future work that is planned. Often, the intake assessment involves my having conversations with other staff, board members, and/or stakeholders within or associated with the organization. As part of the intake assessment, I ask about hopes, fears, and concerns, and I ask how patterns of oppression and white supremacy show up within the organization. After the intake assessment, I make recommendations to the organization about what is needed; my recommendations routinely include monthly affinity groups.

If I recommend that what needs to take place is a level-setting and consciousness-raising training focused on shared language, shared history, and a shared understanding of personal, interpersonal, institutional, and cultural racism for staff, leadership, and other stakeholders, affinity groups are routinely part of the consciousness-raising process. After the consciousness-raising process, I work with organizations to set up equity teams to continue to steward the racial equity work. More often than not, the equity team will make a recommendation to create and secure facilitation for affinity groups within the organization.

Sometimes white and BIPOC affinity groups are set up for leadership, staff, and the board of directors separately; other times, white and BIPOC affinity groups are set up to include people from different roles who perform different functions and are at different levels of leadership within the organization. In either case, it is important to consider how power based on role, function, social location, and positionality within the institution might affect people's experience with the overall racial equity process or initiative and their experience in affinity groups.

It is very important to take time to build trust in the affinity group and talk about refraining from retribution and attribution. Confidentiality is on the list of community-care practices. In an organizational setting, people who participate in a BIPOC affinity group may be concerned that their colleagues in attendance will not maintain confidentiality and that things will be shared outside the space that might negatively affect someone in the BIPOC affinity group. In groups where there are participants with different levels of positional power, it is important to work to create a culture within the group where what is shared within the group isn't used against those sharing—for example, in performance evaluations, or brought up at a later time by a supervisor who wants to use the comments their supervisee said against them. As you facilitate affinity groups within organizations, you need to take time to share the consequences that could occur if confidentiality is broken, particularly within the context of an institutional affinity group. You may also need the support of leadership or some other accountability group in place within the organization to enforce the consequences if someone breaks confidentiality. You will want to make space for affinity group participants to talk about how they will be accountable to one another by honoring the community-care practice of confidentiality, and really all of the community-care practices, as well as the larger goal of supporting one another and interrupting white supremacy, racism, and the different behaviors that manifest from internalized racial oppression.

When an organization embarks on an initiative or process intended to make its organization more racially equitable, it is important for everyone within the organization to be involved in the process. That said, when leadership requires everyone to participate, it can cause resentment and frustration for some people. Most often these feelings arise for those who have less power in the organization, for white-bodied people who do not understand why the organization has embarked on a process focused on racial equity, and for staff of color who are exhausted and do not see how any efforts made to move the organization to become an anti-racist or more equitable organization will make a difference.

An important part of the process of creating equity in an organization is to be clear about the intention for the work and to take direction from those most affected by white supremacy—BIPOC people. This is especially important given the lived-learned dynamic I wrote about in chapter 1. White-bodied people are learning about how to dismantle racism while we as BIPOC people are living in a white supremacy culture and experiencing racism on a daily basis, often multiple times a day. As part of preparing the staff to go through a racial equity process that includes affinity groups, the staff must be given some explanation as to why the organization has chosen to move through a racial equity process, why it has chosen this moment to do so, and what the intended outcome might be as well as what level of participation is expected from the employees of color. Clarity about these things can help decrease any confusion about the intention for the work and the expectations for people of different racial identities and roles within the organization. You may need to provide coaching to leadership or whoever is communicating to the whole organization about the racial equity efforts to support them in clearly articulating intentions and goals.

Another part of the preparation is explaining what the racial equity process will entail—whether this includes consciousness-raising, an equity plan, ongoing affinity groups, or something else. People need to know what to expect and also to expect the unexpected. People need to know that things may change depending on what arises as the racial equity process moves forward. People, and in particular People of Color, must know where they have agency. Do they have the agency to opt out of a training or affinity group? What are the consequences if they do not participate? Who will enforce these consequences? What specific power dynamics must you be aware of as you work to build an accountability structure for a racial equity process? Especially when people have different levels of responsibility and racial identities?

If you are working with a BIPOC leader within an organization who is going to mandate BIPOC participation in affinity groups, encourage them to take time to build relationships with their employees and ask what is most needed. Do the employees want to meet on-site or off-site? Do people want to spend time building relationships (which feels like an essential part of affinity groups) or are people more focused on shifting institutional structures within the organization that create barriers to equity? These two things are not mutually exclusive; focusing on one or the other has a different feel to it in an affinity group taking place within an organization. How might internalized racial oppression coupled with the positional power held by People of Color within the organization affect people's experience in the affinity group?

Another consideration is the communication between white and BIPOC affinity groups taking place within the organization, if there is such affinity group work. Much of this depends on the intention of the equity work within the institution: if the organization is working on an organization-wide initiative to create a more equitable organization, it is important that the racial affinity groups have some sort of protocol for communicating with and updating one another about the work they are doing. If an equity team is being developed or is already in existence in the organization, there should be representatives from both racial affinity groups on the equity team. The equity team meetings can be a place for participants to share about the work they are doing in their specific affinity groups and to share questions and needs, or for the BIPOC affinity group to make recommendations about what they need from the white affinity group and their white-bodied colleagues.

There are constraints specific to organizations that are not usually present when facilitating community affinity groups. Within organizations that are engaged in a longer-term equity process of which affinity groups are a part, there is usually a budget for racial equity work. Even though there may be a budget for the work, often the work is added on to people's other job responsibilities without any relief from work duties or any renegotiation of responsibilities or compensation. For many of us, we don't feel like we have an option to involve ourselves in racial equity work because we are the ones at stake if white supremacy persists. If you are a BIPOC employee within an institution who has been tasked with facilitating the BIPOC affinity group, you can ask what the budget is for your facilitation time and how the BIPOC employees who will participate in the group will be compensated. I don't just mean financial compensation. Will time off be given to BIPOC employees to take care of themselves after they participate in a racially mixed consciousness-raising process? Will BIPOC employees be afforded time off after participating in a BIPOC affinity group? You might also ask for funding for food for the affinity groups, materials, guest speakers, and off-site educational or personal development activities as well.

As previously mentioned, institutions have rules, protocols, and policies that communities do not. Within organizations, there is a way things are done, and this can limit what people can do in BIPOC affinity groups. I do not mention this to discourage you if you are a BIPOC facilitator leading BIPOC affinity groups in your own or another organization. I mention this here to speak realistically about the limitations of structures that we, BIPOC people, didn't create. Part of what we need to do as facilitators *and* BIPOC people is to find a way to access freedom within the context of an organization. When we are meeting within affinity groups in organizations, we need to be strategic, creative, and, as one of my old bosses used to say, subversive.

Lisa Anderson leads a program called the Sojourner Truth Leadership Circle. The program is focused on Black people who identify as or have been socialized as women. Her program takes place in an affinity group because of the people for whom the program was set up. Given that she leads this program within the context of an organization, and because of how white supremacy has become institutionalized in most organizations, Lisa has had to work hard to explain to various levels of leadership that the methodology of bringing Black women together and building relationship with one another is valuable and valid work.

I received pushback, mainly from men within the organization. They didn't like the self-care language and pushed back about language that derives from a radical Black women's space, in particular Audre Lorde. I knew the way

*my program, which was an affinity group by design, had weight underneath
it rooted in womanist and Black feminist principles. But I had to fight for
recognition of that weight. I knew my fight had to do with the outward-facing
appearance of our organization developing a program solely focused on Black
women and how this might land with white funders. I knew I was building a
program for Black women. . . . Somebody could say, are you working? Because,
you know, we come together [for our group meetings] and we check in, and the
check-ins are deep. We are each other's squad, and we take as much time as it
takes to hear the stories of how we are. We hear about where we're struggling
or where we're doing well. If we meet every week, and often an hour of that
meeting time is checking in and just saying here I am, see me tell my story.
It's world making to be in each other's lives that way. There is a space of rest
and respite.*

—LISA ANDERSON

Even if an organization has approved BIPOC affinity groups, we
might be met with resistance once we meet in our affinity group. In these
moments, we must come up with a way to create a unique solution in a
context that wants us to be anything but unique and instead wants us to
conform to white supremacy standards, which have become institutionalized in almost every organization.

I was leading an ongoing BIPOC affinity group in a white-led organization whose mission was wellness and well-being, in particular for people
who have been marginalized by systems of dominance and superiority.
Many of the BIPOC affinity group members were frustrated with their
white-bodied colleagues who didn't seem to understand the importance of
the racial equity work and would become easily overwhelmed by it. The
BIPOC affinity group was also concerned that leadership was not fully
invested in the racial equity work.

When I first met with the group, the members didn't seem to know
each other well, and some were apathetic because they had been asking
for change related to dismantling racism and working toward racial equity
for quite a long time. Given my understanding of the role of relationship
in healing our racialized trauma and internalized oppression, my response
to the group's frustration was to focus on relationship building. We spent
the first six months building relationship with one another in this affinity group.

Every agenda was about more deeply connecting with one another and listening to different perspectives and experiences within the organization. By the sixth month of meeting with this group, they seemed closer and ready to move on to strategy. They wanted to respond to leadership and ask them to be accountable to the racial equity process and to share with everyone the reason why the organization was engaged in this work. They also wanted leadership to put in accountability measures to ensure people's participation and commitment to the racial equity work. Because the affinity group members had strengthened relationships with one another, they were better positioned to come up with creative solutions and strategies to call leadership to be accountable. This included asking leadership to create an accountability plan for everyone within the organization, particularly white-bodied folks, to be responsible to the equity work the organization had chosen to do.

They chose two people from their affinity group who had a bit more positional power than others in the organization to schedule a meeting with the leadership team. They made a list of recommendations and shared them with the leadership team and asked for a response within two weeks. In their list of recommendations, they shared what they felt needed to be communicated to the full staff and they also suggested a system of accountability, which included placing a commitment to equity work in each person's job description, to be reviewed yearly during performance reviews and evaluations.

The affinity group advised the leadership team on specific language to use in the job descriptions. They also suggested creating an advisory board consisting of stakeholders outside of the community who had experience with and an interest in seeing the organization become more equitable. The advisory board would be created to make sure leadership was accountable and doing what they said they would do to make the organization more equitable. This strategy ensured that leadership not only would communicate with staff about the importance of the equity work but also would be accountable for being in integrity with the values focused on equity by making significant change within the organization and taking direction from the advisory board.

This all began by focusing on building relationships to build a better support system for folks of color who were employees in that organization. Relationship building is one of the biggest antidotes to white supremacy.

This is just one example of what can happen within organizations. When we gather, share, and connect, especially in an institution that has been constructed to keep us apart and isolated, we can make a vital change.

When considering these dynamics, you might reflect on whether you've seen BIPOC affinity groups housed in organizations be creative, strategic, and subversive, and how they've engaged in these processes. Even if you follow all of these suggestions, there really is no way around the potential frustration that might be expressed by People of Color in an organization who are made to participate in a racial equity process. The considerations I have shared will help lessen or mitigate some of the frustrations but will not completely stop them from emerging. So many of us have been deeply concerned about what is happening to us and unable to disrupt and dismantle racism because this truly is the work white-bodied people need to do. Of course we have work to do together, centered on how we can more fully support and create a culture of care for one another within the context of an organization and beyond.

Although communities are less constrained in the ways Stephanie mentioned—because they are not bound to policies, practices, and protocols that exist in organizations—they still face constraints and challenges. Sometimes these constraints originate in the reason affinity groups are coming together, in resources for facilitation of and participation in affinity groups, in community dynamics, and in a lack of a clear understanding of why folks are meeting in affinity groups. Facilitating a one-time community-based affinity group will feel different than facilitating an ongoing one. Often, I facilitate one-time community affinity groups to provide a space for healing in the aftermath of another one of our lives being taken by white supremacy because of our unjust policing system, to make a space for us to process our racialized trauma, or to strategize in response to a community of color's wish to build relationship and unity with one another. Sometimes these one-time affinity groups lead to an ongoing group, and other times, they meet once and do not meet again.

When I offer an ongoing community affinity group, these groups often come together as part of a larger organizing effort within a community to respond to a racially unjust incident or a history of racially unjust incidents. Of course, communities have their issues and different positional power and roles that can create barriers. Still, in general, there is more freedom in community affinity groups because people come from different spaces within the community and do not carry the same baggage that can come from working with people in an organization.

People coming to either a one-time or an ongoing affinity group may be coming into the affinity space with different levels of experience and different understandings of racism and white supremacy. You may spend more time doing some level-setting in a community affinity group than in an organizational affinity group, especially if folks within a particular community have not been in a shared process to level-set and develop a shared understanding of personal, institutional, and cultural racism. Community affinity groups aren't mandatory; people show up for the group because they want to, but they may also have different hopes for the affinity group or needs they want to be met. As the facilitator, you can do an intake assessment with each group member prior to starting the affinity group, or you might spend the first part of your first session with the community group gathering information about their needs and hopes for their participation in the affinity group. It can be more difficult to build relationships in a community affinity group, particularly if people drop in and out and do not regularly attend. You could speak to the impact on the group and ultimately their organizing efforts if participants cannot consistently show up and remain in collaboration with the affinity group. You can come up with a system that will keep group participants informed of what the affinity group is focused on in the event someone or a few people have to miss one or a few sessions.

Something else to consider is when BIPOC affinity groups are happening in community alongside white affinity groups. For years, an organizing group offered racial equity trainings in my community and created an anti-racist organizing circle that was racially mixed. As part of their work, they set up affinity groups for people who had been through their racial equity trainings. The purpose of these affinity groups was to work toward taking collective action against racism in our community. The organizing group had identified and created racial equity goals in collaboration with the community and had developed a plan for our community. They invited various community organizers, government agency personnel, elected officials, schoolteachers and administrators, and police and court officers to take their racial equity training. The organizing group wanted to engage these entities and institutions in their dismantling work as a strategy toward dismantling racism within the community.

The white-bodied and BIPOC associated with this organizing group all had some stake in the work of making the community anti-racist, raising awareness of racial inequities that existed in the community, and living into their right role in the work of dismantling racism within our community. The BIPOC and white affinity groups, and the facilitators of these groups, were in constant communication about what they were working on or what was needed at a particular time. This community group is still connected. They continue to offer racial equity trainings today and lead organizing efforts nationwide that inspire communities to organize against white supremacy and racism. This was a powerful testament to what can happen when a community comes together and organizes to make a change. (We will explore more about collective action in chapter 11.)

Whether in a community or organization, we must come up with ways to respond to the interesting challenges both contexts can present. This means we must tap into our genius and the genius of the group to make the needed change we want to see in the world. I believe this is what we as People of Color are always asked to do: *dream outside of white supremacy's constraints.*

To conclude this chapter, I provide some questions on which you can reflect about community and organizational affinity groups.

REFLECTION QUESTIONS

- In your experience of participating in or facilitating affinity groups, what differences have you noticed, depending on the context (an organization or community) in which the affinity group is taking place?
- What different strategies might you use while leading an affinity group in an organization as opposed to leading an affinity group in a community setting?
- If BIPOC people within an organization that is engaged in a racial equity process seem apathetic about the process—for the reasons mentioned earlier in this chapter related to why BIPOC people might not want to participate in affinity groups or racial equity processes taken on by the organization in which they work— how might you meet their apathy? How would you respond to their apathy?

- If you have participated in affinity groups held within the community and outside an organization, how have you seen these affinity groups lead to more unified organizing efforts to dismantle racism and strengthen relationships between BIPOC people? If you have not participated in affinity groups held within the community and outside an organization, how you do imagine that community affinity groups could lead to more unified organizing efforts to dismantle racism while strengthening relationships between BIPOC people?

CHAPTER 9

EVERYTHING IS NOT PERFECT

*If everything was perfect, you would
never learn and you would never grow.*

—BEYONCÉ KNOWLES,
Interview magazine, 2013

A S YOU KNOW BY NOW, facilitating is a practice, one that is most certainly about embracing our and others' imperfections and responding to complexities, nuances, and challenges as best you can when you can. Facilitating anti-racism trainings, racial equity work and practice, and BIPOC affinity groups has been some of the most rewarding work I have ever done in my life. My soul is fed by the work I do to dismantle racism and create conditions for our collective liberation, including facilitating affinity groups. My heart is fed by reimagining our world, a world in which we can all be truly free. It is healing to be with people who, like me, are trying to figure out how to heal wounds that we didn't create for ourselves—wounds that the white supremacy culture created for us. In this chapter, I share themes and some additional challenges that may arise as you facilitate BIPOC affinity groups. I share these challenges not to take away from how rewarding and life-affirming it can feel to facilitate BIPOC affinity groups, but so you feel as fully prepared as you can when you take on the role of facilitating and holding space for such profound and life-changing work.

FALL IN LINE AND FOLLOW THE RULES

When I first attended graduate school to become a social worker, I worked as a social worker in a nursing home. Up until that point, I had not yet been through my first dismantling racism training, or really many racial equity trainings, but something in me was already feeling the pull to hold affinity space for BIPOC people. My supervisor at the nursing home was a Black man. He was very kind and gentle, and he wanted to play by the rules. Being a social work student and someone who was new to the industry of nursing homes and assisted-living facilities allowed me to notice some things about the system that I believe my supervisor had either learned to live with or didn't notice. The certified nursing aides, most of whom were Black, were underpaid and overworked. This meant that at times our patients were neglected. The two social workers, my boss and I, were there to work with the families and advocate for our patients, and we were often met with resistance from the doctors, who were predominantly white, and the head of the nursing home, who also happened to be a white-bodied individual. The white patients seemed to receive more attention and care from the nursing-home staff. While I have my suspicions about why, all of which have to do with how white supremacy functions, I also know that our elders—both white-bodied and BIPOC—are often thrown away and disregarded by institutions. I don't think many residents at the nursing home were having a good experience or being adequately cared for, and I believe the BIPOC patients experienced subpar care disproportionately, certainly more so than their white counterparts. I brought this up to my boss and a few of the Black certified nursing aides. I learned more than I wanted to about the system, and this propelled me to pull together an affinity group for the Black employees and to bring together some of the Black families of Black patients who were residents at the nursing home.

My boss was very resistant to this idea because he didn't want to bring more attention to us (Black folks) in the organization. He wanted to fall in line and follow the rules. I wanted to burn the whole thing down. We were treating people inhumanely, and this didn't sit right with me at all. I don't think it sat right with my boss, either, but I think he had been conditioned to follow the rules—likely for good reason, such as keeping his job and feeding his family of five. He wanted to move up in the field of social work within elder care. I had no question about his ethics or care for the residents. He had been around longer than I had, and I believe he knew the consequences of bucking a system that would much rather have folks stay quiet and in line.

When we stay in line, we uphold systems that harm us, other People of Color, and those less proximal to power. When we stay in line and uphold the status quo and white supremacy ideals and values, we maintain a system that was never designed for our liberation. We keep rigid systems in place that are actively working to oppress us. My boss was upholding white supremacy, and in some ways I was, too, because I continued to work in the nursing home until I graduated a year later. I worked there because I had out-of-state student loans to pay off and didn't have any other way to pay my rent and other expenses. I was not quiet about what was happening within that organization. I did bring together the employees and Black family members of residents to organize and hear more about what they wanted. I also met with the director of the nursing home to tell him my concerns. When I could, I tried to be subversive, and I looked out for the residents as best I could.

UPHOLDING WHITE SUPREMACY NORMS

When we offer anti-racist or racial equity work, including leading and facilitating affinity groups, particularly in organizations but not exclusive to organizations, we will encounter BIPOC people who have consciously and unconsciously assimilated into a white supremacy system and who are upholding patterns of whiteness and white supremacy. As explained in chapter 1, personal, institutional, and cultural racism are all forms we address when we lead affinity groups. BIPOC people may uphold a white supremacy system by going along with or supporting institutional practices and policies that further exclude, underserve, oppress, and exploit other BIPOC people. People of color may discount how racism impacts them individually and collectively to survive within an organization where they currently work. BIPOC people might try to disrupt a process meant to create conditions for BIPOC people to be free and liberated because of what they have internalized about who they are as a person of color and because they have internalized that white is superior.

Not all skinfolk are kinfolk. Working with folks who are, I would say, assimilated, but actually, the term that's coming to mind is like conditioned. We're all conditioned. Some of us are more deeply conditioned. Some of us are more deeply into our unlearning journey, but it's been really challenging to sit with folks who are actively and consciously upholding white supremacy, whiteness because they feel like it's worked for them. And then challenging other people, denigrating and challenging them and asking why they're not adhering to whiteness.

—STEPHANIE GHOSTON PAUL

DISRUPT THE HEALING

In your work and practice as an affinity group facilitator, expect to encounter some BIPOC who question your methodology and credibility and want to disrupt the healing and transformational work you are doing within the context of a BIPOC affinity group. This could show up as someone breaking the confidence of the affinity group and reporting things to an organization's human resources department that will have a detrimental effect on the staff who are BIPOC. This might show up as folks looking the other way and keeping their heads down. This might show up as folks coming into an affinity group and wondering why we need to meet and organize together against white supremacy. It could show up as someone sharing a belief that reverse racism is real because they do not truly understand the definition of racism, which suggests that BIPOC people can be all sorts of things like mean and prejudiced, but not racist.

DEFENDING THE INSTITUTION

Years ago, when I was an elected official in North Carolina, we had a community forum in response to the murder of Michael Brown and the protests taking place in Ferguson, Missouri. Our police chief at the time was a Black man and had been in the role of police chief for less than a year. During the forum, the elected officials, including me, had agreed with one another to mainly sit back and listen to the community versus speaking up and guiding the conversation. Our police chief sat in the front of the room, and people started to ask him questions. They asked about what the police department was going to do to decrease racial profiling, and they shared questions regarding implicit bias and racial equity training for members of the police department. As the police chief responded to the questions, I watched him and listened to his responses. I also found myself biting my tongue; at one point, I had to sit on my hands to keep myself from talking.

I had great respect for the police chief and acknowledged the difficult position he was in at the time. He was the police chief and a Black man. He sat in front of a racially mixed group answering questions from concerned, angry, and grieving community members. When he responded to the question about racial profiling, he said something like "We don't have a problem with racial profiling here. Our police officers aren't racist." He went on to say, "Well, I'm afraid when I'm out of uniform in other towns." This let me know that he was in a pickle of sorts. He was acknowledging his Blackness and how that placed him in harm's way at times, especially when he was out of uniform in other towns and when it wasn't visible to others that he was a police officer. He also wanted to protect his officers and he wanted to uphold an image that the police department wasn't racist. His answer to the question led community folks—Black, white-bodied, and Latinx—to a heated discussion about whether or not the town was racist.

I couldn't sit on my hands any longer and proceeded to get up. I spoke to the community and said, "We do not need to be in a conversation about whether or not our town is racist or whether or not the police department is racist. The system of policing is racist, and we cannot separate the history of policing from how present-day policing operates, nor can we separate what happened in Ferguson, Missouri, from what could happen in our town." I wasn't interested in having a conversation about whether or not white-bodied people, city government, or police departments were racist. To me, that was a distraction from the task at hand. The purpose of the community forum was to provide a space for folks to share, heal, and talk about a system of accountability that needed to be put in place to attempt to ensure police offers were adequately trained in implicit bias, anti-racism, and other strategies that might prevent tragedies like the murder of Michael Brown.

While this setting wasn't an affinity group, similar challenges might come up while facilitating affinity groups—you might be faced with the question of defending an institution at the expense of the People of Color who work within it or who are part of the community that organization serves. A way to respond to this is to acknowledge the competing values and needs that might be present for people in your affinity group. You can rely on your community-care practices, and you might also set some expectations about a focus for the affinity group. For example, if someone in the affinity group says, "I don't know why we are spending time on this, nothing is wrong. Our director [who is white-bodied] takes care of us, and there isn't a problem with racism here." You can remind the group participant to speak from their personal experience to avoid generalizing. You can take some time to invite a couple of people in the group to share their experiences in the organization, and you can remind people of the purpose of the group, which is not to decide whether or not racism or internalized racism is real. The affinity group aims to support participants to understand better how things like internalized racial inferiority, white supremacy, and racial trauma affect individuals in the group and the collective.

If this kind of situation emerges in a community affinity group, people may express that they don't see the problem, and that they don't understand why we would spend time talking about racism in a BIPOC affinity group when there are other pressing community concerns. You can use a strategy similar to the one you would use in an organizational affinity group. You can invite folks to share why they are in attendance and to share their perspective and experiences of racism in the community. You can remind participants of the purpose of the affinity group and practice seeing how things like white supremacy, racial trauma, and internalized oppression play out in the community.

Another dynamic that could emerge as you facilitate BIPOC affinity groups is the presumption of unity.

> *Sometimes there is an assumption or presumption of unity in these spaces [BIPOC affinity groups], and it's a delicate balance of, we want to be unified, but we are still different. So we don't all have to believe the same thing or even take the same stance, but how do we move our momentum forward as a group? And that's been a challenge, I think, especially for Black folks in particular, but for other folks of color; not being unified is seen as you're not part of the pack. Like, you're not woke enough, or you don't know the language or whatever.*
>
> —STEPHANIE GHOSTON PAUL

OUR DIFFERENT LIVED EXPERIENCES

Many of us come together in affinity groups to build relationships with one another and to come into a place of unity. We are coming from different spaces, identities, backgrounds, places of work, and sometimes communities. We shouldn't assume we are all on the same page or share the same beliefs just because we are coming together in an affinity group. We also do not need to weaponize our understanding of language, history, or the analysis of power. When we weaponize knowledge, and especially from a space of believing we know and others do not, white supremacy thrives; we do not.

As a facilitator, you can acknowledge the reality that folks are coming from different places with various lived experiences of systemic racism. It is likely that the experiences people bring into the group with them will not always overlap with those of everyone else in the group. You can also normalize that it takes time to build relationships and come into unity. Unity may not be the explicit goal of the affinity group you are leading, but understanding one another better may be. Through the use of the community-care agreements, an explanation of the assumptions, and your skillful facilitation, you can encourage the group to meet people where they are, understanding that we all have things to learn.

MIXED ROOTS

Another dynamic that may present itself in an affinity group you are facilitating is that sometimes folks who are biracial, white, and of color will attend your affinity group for BIPOC people. I explored this situation in chapter 5 when I discussed separating a racially mixed group into affinity groups. This may happen for various reasons. Perhaps there are just two facilitators, you (if you identity as BIPOC and not biracial) and a white facilitator. You may not have a biracial facilitator who can hold a space for biracial folks. Perhaps you have a biracial facilitator, but a biracial participant identifies more as BIPOC than biracial and wants to come to your affinity group. A biracial participant may not feel comfortable going to the white affinity group.

My experience facilitating BIPOC affinity groups that include biracial people is that often they are very respectful of the fact that the space may feel tenuous for them and the other group participants who do not identify as biracial. I do know that if folks who are biracial haven't had a space to process in a setting like an affinity group prior to my affinity group offering, they may feel relief when afforded the space to share. They may want to process all of their feelings about being biracial in a setting where

I as the facilitator cannot speak to this particular experience from my own experience. The group may not be able to either.

This can cause tension, and it is up to you to hold the space in a way that honors the biracial participant, keeping in mind how the racial hierarchy functions, and that makes space for folks who are not biracial to process and share. This is not easy to do, but it is possible. If we are holding a BIPOC affinity group versus an affinity group broken into groups of Black, Asian, Latinx, Indigenous, or biracial people, it is our job to create as much of an open and affirming space as possible. We do not want to create barriers that further exclude people; we want to make space for people to be in a way that the world—because of how white supremacy functions—doesn't always allow. We can rely on our community-care agreements and practices, skillful facilitation, and facilitator techniques to create this kind of space.

TIME AND TENDERNESS

An additional dynamic that may present a challenge in affinity groups is the reality that you are opening people up in a time-limited process, be that in an organization or a community facilitation. I touched on this in chapter 8 when I described the dynamic of offering an affinity group within the context of a workday and the importance of supporting group participants in their transition out of the affinity group and onto other work tasks.

> *Affinity group spaces can be tender. They can be sacred; they can be places of deep medicine. It's about the depth of holding space for folks. Many Black folks that I'm in community with are numbing themselves, parts of themselves to get through the day and to be in a space where you can open up. And there are people who understand affinity groups open up people and that we can't be together all day, every day. It's a challenge to hold this. Affinity group participants might not have elsewhere to go to share about their experience as a Black person or person of color. And how do we hold the space carefully, easefully, and responsibly because you and the group participants have to go back out into the world?*

—STEPHANIE GHOSTON PAUL

I feel the tenderness created in affinity spaces so deeply. I led a yoga asana and meditation class for women of color for about a year. We would meet weekly for seventy-five minutes to share, move, breathe, and build community with one another. One time I was leading a rest practice, and I sat and watched the women in the space resting in what seemed to me to be a peaceful manner. I sat there with grief in my heart because I knew that, after the period of rest, I would have to send these women back into the world of white supremacy. I felt as if I was setting up an experience whereby I invited women of color into a space where they could more fully be themselves, only to send them out into the world, a world that prioritizes the ideals of white supremacy, not the lives of women of color. It pained me to bring them out of rest and prepare them to leave class that evening.

I have experienced a similar feeling of grief in my heart while facilitating affinity groups in other contexts. I invite people into a space, make room for them to be themselves more fully, and then close the group and send them on their way. There is no way around this dynamic other than to speak to it with the group and trust that what we offer as facilitators is more aligned with liberation and care than is the white supremacy culture in which we live. This is one of the hazards we must face as we take on the honorable and sacred duty of facilitating BIPOC affinity groups.

Something that helps me with this dynamic is to remember that the moments of rest, or moments when someone gets to share, cry, be held, be witnessed, and be cared for in response to the ways white supremacy is beating them up physically, emotionally, mentally, psychically, and spiritually are salve moments. They are truly medicinal. The affirming environment I can create as a BIPOC facilitator might be the only affirming space someone has. This lessens my heart pains a bit and allows me to continue to offer what I know we need to heal. Space. Rest. Time. Relationship. Connection. Love. Affirmation. For our brilliance to be recognized and uplifted; our pain to be witnessed—our suffering to be held in space with others and not on our own.

WHEN WE FEEL TRIGGERED

I wrote about self-care for yourself as a facilitator in chapter 6. The final challenge I want to share in this chapter relates to self-care and what our options are when we feel triggered or grabbed by something that happens in our affinity group. We are deeply affected by everything that affects the participants in our affinity group. We move through a world that devalues us because of our race. We feel brokenhearted about what is happening to us, to those who share our racial identity, and to other People of Color.

During your tenure facilitating BIPOC affinity groups, you will feel as brokenhearted as the people who choose to come to the groups you facilitate. The tenderness they feel will likely remind you of the tenderness you have felt. The fear they express when recounting stories of how our lives are taken and our babies are stolen from us will resonate with the fear you yourself have felt or currently feel. The rawness group participants will express in response to the news of the day, which might include the loss of another Black or Brown person to police brutality, or babies being taken away from their families at the border, or unjust policies in schools to keep children from learning the real truth about critical race theory and our shared history, will be rawness you feel on your skin. Most if not all of the things people will bring up in your affinity group will be things you have felt, worried about, or grieved.

This might be the greatest challenge of all: learning how to tend the group while tending your own broken heart. In the moments when I feel overcome with emotion and brokenhearted while facilitating affinity groups, I reveal my heartbreak. I do not do this so the group can take care of me, although I am part of the group even though I am facilitating the group. I reveal my heartbreak because it is the most authentic thing I can do when I feel grabbed, grief-stricken, and heartbroken. By doing this, I make space for the group to share their hearts more fully with myself and each other. Because you will have felt most of what group members share with you and the group, it is important to consider what you will do when you feel overcome with emotion while facilitating. It is equally important to consider how you will care for your heart.

This reminds me of the assumption presented in chapter 1—this work isn't easy, and we have to do it anyway. We do. We have to, and it is deeper than work. It is our lives. When we facilitate, we are listening to people share something that has also likely touched us in some way. We must learn how to take care of ourselves as we do this vital and necessary work.

- What might it feel like for you to reveal your brokenheartedness to an affinity group you are facilitating?
- What resources are available to you to hold your heart and all it is moving through at this time?

- What fears do you have about sharing your emotions with a group you are facilitating?
- What gift might you offer a group by sharing your authentic emotions and self with them?
- Why is it important to bring our full hearts into the work of facilitating BIPOC affinity groups?

These are some other themes and challenges to think about as you facilitate BIPOC affinity groups. I want to remind you that, more often than not, the rewards outweigh the challenges when facilitating BIPOC affinity groups. I hope you receive rewards tenfold from the work and practice you put into holding space for yourself and other BIPOC people.

CHAPTER 10

THE ROLE OF RITUALS

A ritual is an action performed by our body in connection with our spirit.
—SHERENE CAULEY, quoted in Michelle Cassandra Johnson, *We Heal Together: Rituals and Practices for Building Community and Connection*

THERE IS A BELIEF in some spaces and some people's minds that rituals are complex and that we must have crystals, a magic wand, and a special degree to engage in or facilitate rituals. I believe working with rituals is much simpler than this. Every time we form a circle with intention, we are involved in a ritual. Every time we open and close a space in a particular way, we are involved in a ritual. Every time we pause in a circle to let whatever was just spoken land or have room to breathe, we are, in effect, engaged in a ritual. Rituals are routines. They are practices done with reverence. They are sacred, central to our healing as BIPOC people individually and collectively, and part of what will bring us back into a place of embodiment as we heal the scars we have due to white supremacy and racism.

My first memory of actively participating in a ritual was in church. I grew up in a Black Baptist church. Every Sunday we would attend church and move through the rituals of prayer, song, and Scripture and be reminded that there was a source much more significant than us, God. We did this every Sunday to wade through the grief we held in our hearts and move through the trauma that comes from living in a white supremacy culture. We gathered together in community every Sunday to heal the scars we held within our bloodlines, spirits, hearts, minds, bodies, and psyches. Scars that come from living in a world that would rather we not exist.

The ritual of attending church each Sunday, and the rituals shared while moving through the church ceremony, supported Black people and communities in remembering the countless acts of racism that hurt us but didn't break us.

> "We retain a memory of our injuries, whether they are physical or psychological, even after the injury has healed and scarred over. Where scar tissue formed, we can, from time to time, be reminded of the hurt. This is especially true of our deepest wounds. . . . Racial wounding is painful and approaching those wounds risks reopening them because race-based stress and trauma linger. But our emotional scars are the marks that tell a story of times when life really hurt us but did not break us."
>
> —GAIL PARKER, *Restorative Yoga for Ethnic and Race-Based Stress and Trauma*

My favorite part of the church service was the singing. When the choir sang, it was as if the vibration in my body and the entire church building was transformed. Through song I could feel something bigger than me moving through and around me. The resonant hums of church members on either side of me and the amens that resounded throughout church service during song and sermon made me know the experience of what it is to embody faith—the belief in myself, in us, our ancestors, and God. Faith that we were more than white supremacy told us. Faith that our dreams could transcend the reality that white supremacy held no dreams for us and instead, actively wished our genius and brilliance away.

Long since I stopped attending the church in which I grew up, I have sat in so many circles that have reminded me of the kind of faith I experienced in church. Affinity groups have been some of the most powerful of these circles. I have sat in affinity groups that have woven rituals throughout the entire session, reminding us that we aren't the negative things the world tells us about who we are. These rituals have brought me and groups in which I have been a participant or facilitated back to the truth of who we are.

We are Love.
We are Light.
We are God.
We are Magic.
We are Brilliant.

We are Beautiful.
We are Truth.
We are Justice.
We are Soft.
We are Strong.
We are all our Ancestors Dreamt of.
We are Everything we Need to be.

Even though white supremacy has tried to take all of who we are, we are everything we need to be.

CULTURAL APPROPRIATION

Before moving into specific suggestions for rituals you can offer in affinity groups, I want to talk about cultural appropriation and the reality for so many of us of having been separated from our cultural rituals and practices. The church was such a healing space for me and the rituals offered there could be traced back to my lineage of singing in the cotton field, jumping the broom at a wedding, baptisms in the James River, and prayer—these make me long to know many other from my ethnicity and lineage.

Until very recently I identified as Black, but I wasn't sure exactly where I was from. After taking a 23andme test, I found out I am 80 percent West African and 20 percent Irish. I look and strongly identify as Black, and in looking at me, you would never know I had any Irish roots at all. I long to know more about the rituals rooted in my blood lineage—the rites of passage, the songs that are sung for births, and rituals practiced to honor someone's transition from the earthly to the heavenly realm. I yearn to move through ceremonies that bring in elemental magic—earth, air, fire, water, the above and the below. I crave knowledge about rituals from my lineage that mark the passing of time and the seasonal changes, the call for rain so that the crops can grow and the animals and people can flourish and quench their thirst. I want to know more about these rituals, and the reason I do not know more is because white supremacy stole people from their homeland and stole cultural practices and traditions, forbidding the practice of rituals.

White supremacy, with a sense of entitlement, appropriates rituals and commodifies them for capitalist gain. In so many ways, white supremacy has taken rituals like the Day of the Dead, yoga, dream catchers, rabbit feet charms, hoodoo, voodoo, and others out of context, without any relationship to the people they come from or the way they were intended to be used or practiced.

As defined in chapter 1, cultural appropriation is extracting or adopting element(s) from one culture without an appreciation for or a relationship with that culture. The people taking the element(s) from a culture to which they are not connected often are in a dominant position within dominant culture or are a representation of dominant culture. There is usually material, emotional, physical, or spiritual gain for the person or people engaging in cultural appropriation. In other words, dominant culture profits from cultural appropriation, which causes suffering materially, emotionally, physically, and spiritually for people marginalized by dominant culture. As you prepare to lead rituals in your affinity group, you want to be aware of not perpetuating the act of cultural appropriation. In some ways, this might be difficult because we do not always know where we or practices and rituals are from, but we can investigate and ask. My friend and comrade Vivette Jeffries-Logan often encourages people, especially those most proximal to power, to seek to know their lineage and rituals. The act of seeking out information about rituals connected to your lineage is an antidote to white supremacy and capitalism. We are not entitled to rituals and practices that are not directly connected to where we come from. Taking time to deepen your understanding of where you are from and to learn more about cultural traditions connected to your roots is yet another way to dismantle white supremacy. In addition to investigating our own cultural background and rituals, if we are going to offer rituals that aren't directly connected to our lineage in affinity groups, we can ask permission from folks we are in a relationship with who are from a lineage from which we wish to offer. We can invite different people in the group to bring in rituals that are connected to their own culture and lineage.

RITUALS TO PRACTICE IN AFFINITY GROUPS

I have already introduced the ritual of opening and closing groups, taking a breath together, and recentering after a tense moment or pausing when something or someone needs more space. This chapter offers rituals meant to be practiced during the affinity group, rituals for you to move through as you prepare to facilitate an affinity group, and rituals to engage after you have just finished facilitating an affinity group. Before diving into an explanation of certain rituals, I invite you to pause in the ritual of self-inquiry and reflect specifically on your relationship with rituals.

REFLECTION QUESTIONS

- How do you define ritual?
- What rituals do you currently practice?
- What rituals bring you the most healing, rituals that either you facilitate for yourself or have had someone else facilitate for you?
- Are there rituals directly connected to your lineage that you envision bringing into an affinity group?

The Ritual of Presence

We always connect with feelings, gratitude, and intentions. We slow down, especially when we hear that something is happening, somebody died, or someone is sick. We give space, there's a prayer offered up. We don't know what we are going to get when we come together in affinity space. We never know what the cooperative members are holding or what they will say. We will stop the meeting because the business [purpose of the affinity group] is us.

—NATASHA HARRISON

The ritual of presence is about being present to what people might bring into the space with them and what might emerge as the affinity group meeting unfolds. I talked about throwing out the agenda in chapter 6. The ritual of presence is not only about going with the flow of what needs attention as you facilitate; it's also about the ritual of being with one another and everything we might bring into an affinity group. The ritual of presence is pausing to co-hold someone's grief or shock in response to the death of someone or to the transition a group member might be moving through. There are many ways you can call people into presence, many of which have already been described here. The breath. Checking in. Taking time to build connections with one another. Listening.

Affirmation Ritual

There is always music. Always food. Always some dancing. There's always movement. It's important for people to have space around the naming of them, like who they are.

—NATASHA HARRISON

I love, love, love, love affirming that people are supposed to be here, in general, and in the affinity space I do this by saying, "You are supposed to be here." I feel like opening with that just settles people and it's been helpful for biracial people who are wondering, should I be here? It's been helpful for folks who are more deeply conditioned or early on their unlearning journey of releasing internalized oppression. It's been helpful for me. Like I deserve a refuge. Like I deserve this space. Like I deserve to be seen and held. I belong here and I think there are so many spaces where we're, we're told we don't belong. So just starting that way, I feel like it's really special.

—STEPHANIE GHOSTON PAUL

This ritual is simple and profound. You can begin with a moment of silence or meditation and then welcome folks into the space by affirming that the affinity group is a space for them. You can do this just as Stephanie does, by saying, "You are supposed to be here. You belong. You deserve a space of refuge. You deserve to be seen and held." You could also have these affirmations written up and placed on posters around the room, or if you are on Zoom, you can say the affirmations aloud and then type them in chat or share your screen and have a slide with the affirmations on them. You can ask the group to repeat the affirmations after you have spoken them. Affirming other BIPOC people's very being is medicine. As we affirm other BIPOC people's very being, we affirm our own being and give ourselves permission to simply be.

Building an Altar

An altar is a place to make offerings and sacrifices, summon energy, honor our ancestors, and give thanks. Altars are places where we lay down our burdens or gather the energy we most need at the time. If I could, I would spend all of my time building altars in groups with people because they bring a level of reverence into spaces that automatically bring us into community and our shared humanity. They slow us down and call us to be intentional with one another and whatever we've chosen to place on the altar.

Altar building is a tradition that can be traced back to many lineages, and taking time to build an altar in your affinity group can be a nice way to begin or end your group. If you want to invite your affinity group to build an altar, you can invite everyone to bring in an object representative of a particular person, topic, or experience. Often, I invite people to bring in an object as a way of introducing themselves to the group. People bring in rocks or gems, photographs, candles, flowers, and sacred texts, to name just a few. One by one, I invite participants to go around the circle and offer their altar object and share something about it. You can give folks a time limit of one minute to share something about their altar item. After they complete their share, instruct them to place their item on the altar. If you are moving through this ritual on Zoom, you can ask everyone to share their item and to place it in a sacred space wherever they are. After everyone has shared, you can ask the group to take a moment in silence to honor what has been shared and offered in the space.

In preparation for your affinity group, you might let participants know in advance that they are invited to help build an altar by bringing an object that is representative of an item they choose from the following list.

THEMES FOR ALTAR BUILDING
- The participant's name
- Someone who is an emotionally, physically, mentally, and spiritually healthy or well ancestor or mentor—this could be a teacher or even something from the natural world, such as an animal
- Their hopes for participation in the affinity group
- A point of refuge
- What they would like to heal for themselves and/or in their community
- Their fears
- Their questions
- A transition they are moving through
- Their resilience

I find that once the altar is built, it holds powerful energy for the group. It becomes an anchor, both a participant's own object and the collective altar the group has built. Altars almost become another group participant because of the energy they contain. From time to time as you facilitate your affinity group, you can ask people to bring their awareness and attention to the altar as a way of re-grounding them in the space and reorienting them to their object and the altar built by the collective. When the affinity group or process is moving toward a close, you can ask folks to share something they learned in the group, a way they were inspired, or an appreciation or offering to the group as they gather their altar item. If time is tight, you can have them gather their altar item, or if they are on Zoom, bring their awareness back to the item they chose to share with the group and hold and feel its energy for a minute.

If you are meeting with a group over an extended period of time and the affinity group is coming to a close, or if you want to mark the year anniversary of your gathering together as a group or celebrate something within the group, you can ask everyone to bring in something they want to offer to the altar and as a gift to someone in the group. For this activity, you must be in person. Everyone brings in an object representative of whatever prompt you've chosen from the list, or your own prompt. Then they build the altar. One by one, each person in the affinity group is instructed to go up to the altar and choose an object to learn more about. Then, the person who brought it will share a little about it and why they chose to bring it as a gift. You might want to bring a few extra objects in the event a group participant forgets to bring in an item.

A note about altars: if you want to create the altar with some items prior to leading people through the practice of building an altar, please take time to do so. This might be part of what you do to prepare to facilitate, which I will focus on a bit later in this chapter.

I always have a little container holding water and I asked the water to hold the space with me. For earth, I always have some holy dirt here from Chimayo, New Mexico, it's a very sacred place to me. I have usually some different stones that support with the energy. And I always have fire. With wind, it looks different each time I hold space. Sometimes I just invite the group to connect with the breath.

—CELESTÉ MARTINEZ

As Celesté mentioned, you might choose to place something on the altar representative of each element—earth, air, fire, and water. You might also place some other items on the altar prior to inviting participants to add their items. You can explain what is on the altar before asking them to share and add their items.

Storytelling

Just as talking sticks are an old tradition found in many Indigenous lineages, storytelling is also found in many lineages and traditions. There are so many stories for us to tell, and being witnessed as we share stories is such a magnificent experience. As BIPOC people, our stories aren't often centered or we often aren't asked to share our stories. Our stories of wisdom, pride, loss, love, and success have been swept to the side by white supremacy. If you choose to practice storytelling, you can note the importance of being able to share our stories prior to diving into the practice.

There are myriad topics you could invite affinity group participants to share stories about: the origin of their name, an ancestor, a mentor or teacher, their resilience, or the resilience embodied within the people they come from, share something about where they are from, something they are learning at this time, or something they are in deep inquiry about at this time. If you have a large group, you might want to break them into smaller groups of three or four, and then give each group member five minutes to share a story about the topic you've chosen. During the time they tell their story, the other people in their small group will listen to receive their story. Then come back to the large group and debrief how it felt to share their story and be witnessed.

Another way I have brought storytelling to affinity groups and group facilitation is to bring in a short passage from a book or article I have read or am reading. For this, generally, I choose something that is not more than five hundred words. I ask for a volunteer from the group to read a paragraph, and when they have finished reading the paragraph, someone else volunteers to read the next paragraph, and so on until we have completed the reading. Then I invite group participants to journal about the reading. I might offer specific prompts on which they can reflect. Once they have journaled, you can either keep them in the large group to share or invite them into smaller groups to share.

One additional way you can bring stories to your session is to have people reflect on the story they want to share about themselves versus the story dominant culture has created about them. Often I will offer this kind of ritual after we have discussed internalized oppression, and I invite the group to reflect on and write the story they wish to tell about who they are. I give them five minutes to journal about the story or to draw or come up with the expression of their story. Then I break them into small groups to share with one another, after which they debrief in the large group.

Calling In Ancestors

I was in an affinity group late last year and we did some rituals around ancestors. It was super powerful. I think the theme of all of the rituals is how can we sit in our power, call ourselves into the space and honor our traditions, history, and lineages. And every time someone brings forth a ritual that is in alignment with that it is super powerful. We called in ancestors past, present, future, and we did a future visioning of our ancestors five generations in the future and the world that we're creating for them now.

So we were doing some Afrofuturism. We were doing a little magic. It just was really powerful. And every time I've been a part of an ancestor ritual, it's a communal way to experience something that feels really important to folks' identities.

—STEPHANIE GHOSTON PAUL

I have already offered a few prompts about ancestors and how you might bring them into your affinity group. A simple ritual you might guide group participants to move through is the practice of calling in an ancestor they want to be in the space with them. You might open your group with a guided meditation and then invite folks to connect with an ancestor, living or deceased, whom they want to bring into the space. You can have them go around the circle and one by one share the ancestor's name and anything else you might prompt them to share. Some participants might choose to call in more than one ancestor.

This is a powerful practice because even if we believe we are moving through the world alone, we carry all of our ancestors with us, we are living ancestors, and at some point, we will be ancestors who have transitioned from this earthly realm and into another. Uplifting names of ancestors is a reminder that we are in community with our ancestors all of the time. Their blood courses through us, as do their stories of struggle and resilience.

Wisdom

I was a participant in a space where each group participant was instructed to write down a piece of wisdom on a postcard, which would then be mailed to another member of the group. We didn't know who would receive the wisdom we offered or wrote on our postcard. We didn't put our names on the postcard. The group facilitators had the mailing addresses for everyone in the space and let us know we were going to receive a postcard at some point with some wisdom from another group participant. Facilitators addressed and stamped all of the postcards and mailed them out to the group members after the facilitation. This ritual took place over a decade ago, and I still have my postcard.

The one I received says:

Hi friend,

If there is one thing I would like to share or to have you remember, is that you have the ability to create changes and are creating your legacy right now.

In yourself, your agency, your community, and your movement.

What do you want your legacy to be?

You have the power to create and change.

Take care,
Your friend

This postcard sits near my desk and the wisdom on it has served me beyond measure. I love this wisdom ritual because it is the kind that keeps giving, and it's a wonderful way to have what most needs to be reflected back to us, offered from an anonymous friend in the affinity group.

Music

In many cultures, music is a healing balm. I believe in the power of music to transform a space and the people within that space. There are so many ways to bring music into an affinity group for ritual. Earlier I invited you to bring in music for the shaking practice to discharge energy. There are several other ways you can use music in your group. You could bring in music and play a song to open the group. You could bring in music to close the group. You could choose a song that corresponds with the theme of the affinity group or the content you will offer that day and play it, share the lyrics with people, and invite them to journal in response to it—how it made them feel, what it reminds them of, or what it has to do with our resilience as BIPOC people. You could invite affinity group participants to bring in the lyrics of a song that reminds them of their true nature and resilience and share the lyrics in small groups. If you are with the group over a period of time, you could invite an affinity group participant to bring in a two- to three-minute song to share with the large group.

My favorite way to bring in music is through a singing practice. Although I am not a singer, I believe in the power of using our voices. In the yogic tradition, the voice is energetically connected to the throat and heart. Part of what we are doing in our affinity groups is opening and healing the heart. Singing is deep in my familial bloodline and the line of organizers from which I originate. There were so many times when Kenneth Jones, my former colleague with Dismantling Racism Works, or my friend Cynthia Brown burst out into song in our affinity groups.

To bring in ritual through music, I would choose a simple song: something that only has a few lines or just the chorus of a song. You can begin the song and invite participants to join in with you until the practice and ritual feels complete. After you have finished singing, give folks a minute to be in silence if they want to, but don't require silence, because sometimes the heart is so happy after a song, and the practice of singing has passed through and touched the heart so deeply, that people want to laugh because they are feeling joyous. If there is room for a moment of silence, allow it to be after the group finishes audibly singing.

Movement

As Tada Hozumi, a practitioner and steward of cultural somatics, explains, oppression disconnects us from the body and from who we are.

> Oppression disconnects us from the subtle energetic impulses in our bodies that tell us who we really are. We become less human, fixed and rigid. If you take the time to reflect, you will notice that a lack of relational/emotional dexterity is the common thread to all of the "privileged" identities that define oppressive constructs: white, male, rich, able, and so on. Following, inequity isn't privilege itself. That is merely a symptom. Privileges are really institutionalized defense mechanisms, put in place so that privileged identities can avoid processing pain. Oppressive violence is the result of the false privileged self-being triggered into the self-protection reactions of fight/flight/freeze. This is why long-term sustainable social change must fundamentally come from work done at the energetic layer of the body.[1]

White supremacy has many strategies intended to make us forget we have bodies. Strategies such as enslaving, policing, exploiting, and torturing our bodies. All of these vile tactics move us away from any sense of ownership or sovereignty over our bodies. Our bodies are our own, and even though I believe we are more than a physical body, coming back to the physical body is an essential part of our healing journey toward wholeness. Coming back into the body—be that through breath, movement, or other somatic practices—is what we need to do to heal and remember who we are. You can choose to have a full-on dance party in your affinity group or you can guide folks to move on their own or through a few subtle movements to come back into the body. The point is to move people in a way that allows them to remember they are in a body.

Movement can feel very uncomfortable for some people. Even though I am a proponent of movement, I do not move with ease when free movement is offered and there isn't structure. If you choose to incorporate movement into your affinity group, give people the option to opt in or out of the movement practice. If you are meeting with a group for a long period of time and you want to infuse movement into several affinity groups over time, you can start with more structured mindfulness and movement practices such as progressive muscle relaxation, walking meditation, and other guided movement, and then move into more unstructured movement.

Resistance Activity

When I was a facilitator with Dismantling Racism Works (dRworks), we would end our trainings with an activity focused on resilience and building movements of resistance against white supremacy. We would ask folks to think of and bring into the group the name of an organization, poet, or artist, or a practice such as laughter, humor, or rest, or a movement or movement leader or deity or some other force or being that represented resisting the racial hierarchy and construct of race. Once they had thought of the being or force they would be instructed to write it on a sticky note or piece of paper.

They would then get into small groups and share about what came to mind as they called into their awareness the written-down names that represented resistance. Then they would all place their stickies on a wall, and we would invite the entire group to look at the names and take a moment to remember that for every act of racism throughout our history there have been people and forces resisting the divide-and-conquer strategy of white supremacy and racism. You can bring this into your affinity group as described or work with this theme of resistance in some other way. I have found this activity to be an empowering practice for affinity group participants, individually and as a collective. It is so important to remember that we are part of a lineage of energies, people, and forces fighting for our liberation.

There are many other rituals you might choose to bring into your space. If you are going to use a ritual that you learned from someone else, it is important to credit that person. In addition, it is important for you to practice the ritual on your own. You want to have some familiarity with the ritual prior to offering it to a group. That said, sometimes rituals just come to us in the flow of facilitation, so try to have familiarity with it but don't stifle your creative genius if a ritual unexpectedly emerges while you are facilitating.

There are two other rituals that feel important to share: a ritual for you to prepare to facilitate an affinity group, and a ritual for you to complete after the affinity group has concluded. Earlier in this chapter, in the altar-building section, Celesté described having a bowl of water to help hold the space for her. This is an acknowledgment of the fact that she is going to hold space for people and wants some support as she enters into the space and during the facilitation. The other items she described bringing into a space with her, or her space if she is facilitating virtually—items representative of fire, air, water, and earth—are also space-holders and help prepare her to facilitate.

Preparation to facilitate and hold space is key. I usually meditate for a few minutes prior to facilitating. You could take a few deep breaths and call on your ancestors or guides to support you. You could review your intention, the one you were guided to create in chapter 5. You could review the affinity group job description you created. There are many ways to prepare, and I would suggest you choose one and practice it before each affinity group facilitation and see how it feels. You can always change the way you prepare to lead. Having a consistent preparation practice is important.

The other thing to consider is a ritual for you to release the effects of the group when it is over. It is important to find a way to release what has come up in the group so you can transition to your next task, event, or facilitation with ease. There are many techniques you might use to mark the end of your facilitation of an affinity group.

After I hold space, once I kind of settle and I'm away from this virtual tool [Zoom], I always need to lie down. . . . I may not, you know, need to sleep, but I need to lie down and just kind of let it settle into me. I usually need to eat.

—CELESTÉ MARTINEZ

Taking a moment to integrate the experience of having led an affinity group is vital. As you facilitate, your nervous system will most definitely be activated and be in communication with group participants' nervous systems. You are holding things in a different way than the group participants because you are the facilitator. Giving yourself a moment to acknowledge that you have held space, and acknowledging what emerged while you did, can allow you to integrate what you would like to from the experience, honor your facilitation of the group, and release anything that might need to be released from your system—anything you do not want to carry forward with you. This integration and release can result from eating a grounding and nourishing meal, taking a moment to rest, going outside to connect with the natural world, taking some time to meditate, or washing your hands with cool water.

REFLECTION QUESTIONS

- Why is having an integration practice important?
- What practices do you already engage in for integration after you have held space?
- What practices might support you in acknowledging you have held space, honoring your facilitation, and releasing anything that needs to be released from the facilitation?

"Ritual is a powerful tool to maintain our own cohesion, honor our own emotional journey, and acknowledge that we don't know if we will get what we want. It allows us to be with what is while envisioning something different. It lets our minds rest and makes us feel grounded, meaning we are present with the moment and each other to recognize the bigger picture and world around us."

—NAOMI ORTIZ,
Sustaining Spirit: Self-Care for Social Justice

CHAPTER 11

COLLECTIVE LIBERATION AND ACCOUNTABILITY

We are the world, and the world is who we are. And so changing the world means changing ourselves as well as changing those things that are outside of who we are.

—RUBY SALES,
in conversation at the 2020 *CTZN* Summit

IN *A SPACE FOR US* I have explored various themes relating to the facilitation of BIPOC affinity groups. The book offers a multitude of skills needed to hold affinity space for BIPOC people and describes different scenarios you might encounter while facilitating BIPOC affinity groups. In this final chapter, I explore why it is important to have a collective vision for liberation for all, along with some things to consider as we build relationships across racial lines of difference in order to take collective action. In my experience of leading racial equity work in racially mixed organizations and communities who are working together across lines of racial difference to create a more racially just community, it is essential to consider how, together, BIPOC and white-bodied people can support the goal of dismantling racism. As shared in chapter 8, there may be times when you lead an affinity group in the community that is untethered to a more extensive racial equity process. Even in these spaces we are part of a more significant movement that is happening globally to uproot racism and white supremacy.

When I first began leading dismantling racism work, I came into the work as a member of a biracial training collective. There was never a question for our collective about whether or not we were working toward a goal of creating conditions for collective liberation for all. We worked across racial and other lines of difference, and often thought about our appropriate roles and how to be in right relationship based on our social location. The experience of working in a biracial training collective shaped my orientation to the work of dismantling racism and creating racial equity. I understand that everyone may not have come into the work as part of a biracial training team or collective and that your orientation to racial equity work may be different from mine. You might not hold a desire to work across lines of difference.

Many people are leading racial equity work, and there are countless ways to do the work and practice anti-racism. It is most certainly a choice for us to intentionally come into relationship with white-bodied individuals who are working to create a world where racism doesn't exist. It is not a choice we all will make. Even if our intention is to work in BIPOC-only spaces and not across lines of difference, and even though as BIPOC people we have been most harmed by white supremacy, I do believe we can still hold a vision for collective liberation and all work in our own way to get there.

It's a humanity check. If we actually are tied together, if our liberation actually is interwoven, we have work to do together, and we have to wrestle with what we need to wrestle with; we need to build together. We need to build. We need to understand solidarity.

—STEPHANIE GHOSTON PAUL

It is indeed a humanity check when we ask ourselves what collective liberation and action mean to us and why they are important. Are we here for ourselves, other BIPOC people, or collective liberation? These things aren't mutually exclusive, yet I still believe it's an important question to ask. It's important to get clear about what "collective liberation" means and to understand just who we want to be and whom we want to see free.

It is clear to me that white supremacy causes harm to us all, BIPOC and white-bodied people. I am clear that white-bodied individuals and communities are conditioned to see themselves as superior to us. I know white-bodied individuals and communities have terrorized BIPOC communities for centuries and continue to terrorize us. I know we have been tortured, maimed, and oppressed by white-bodied people and communities, and I know that white supremacy has attempted to dampen and snuff out our spirits. I know our babies, dreams, goals, hopes, and desires have been stolen by white supremacy. And I am very clear that white people created white supremacy. I know that white-bodied people may not be invested in our liberation because they can risk not doing anything while we must risk doing everything to claw our way to freedom. I also know that as long as the white supremacy culture continues to condition white-bodied people and communities to believe they are superior, deserving of everything, and entitled to whatever they want, we, as BIPOC people, are going to suffer greatly.

I'm not waiting for white-bodied folks to free me. I am interested in us all getting free because, when that day comes, there will be less harm happening to us and our planet. Our children's children will live in a different world than the one we live in now. The reclamation of our humanity will lead us to be humane to one another and we will have worked to love ourselves into who we can be. Creating this world will take work. It will require us to vision and create a blueprint of our visions and dreams for a world in which everyone is living into our shared humanity. Since you are part of the work as a BIPOC person and affinity group facilitator, it feels important for you to reflect on your vision of collective liberation for all.

REFLECTION QUESTIONS

- What is your vision for collective freedom?
- What actions do we need to take to create a world where we experience collective liberation? What role do you feel white-bodied people and communities need to play?
- Do you want to work across lines of difference to actualize your vision for collective liberation or do you want to hold your vision and work in BIPOC-only spaces?

I recognize your answers to these questions may change over time—you may not know now how you feel about collective liberation. The invitation is to reflect and build some self-awareness of what you believe now, and what questions you have as you enter into or continue on in the role of a BIPOC affinity group facilitator.

What I know to be true about working across racial lines of difference is that white-bodied individuals are going to mess up. Again and again. I know that white-bodied folks might make amends and then ten minutes later make the same mistake they previously made. As mentioned earlier, I know that when I choose to work to dismantle racism in racially mixed spaces where affinity groups are part of the work, and as I work across racial lines of difference, white-bodied people are learning about white supremacy—often at my and our expense.

I expect mistake making, not knowing, and discomfort to arise when things feel messy and unclear, and for white-bodied folks to try to opt out when I need them to lean in. I am not saying these actions are okay, but they are going to happen if you are working across lines of difference or with white-bodied people on a shared vision to dismantle racism. We will have to navigate these dynamics as we work for collective freedom. Of course, my reaction to white-bodied people making mistakes depends on the nature and gravity of the mistakes. My reaction to a white-bodied person's discomfort is often to invite myself and others to be with it; such situations are nuanced, and my response depends on the context and situation. As explored earlier in *A Space for Us*, white supremacy constantly strives to make us feel uncomfortable, all the while prioritizing the comfort of white-bodied people and communities.

Something that helps me with the mistakes white-bodied people make, with their ignorance, and with the discomfort expressed by white-bodied people is the awareness that there are times when I make mistakes, lack awareness and knowledge, and have felt discomfort arise inside me. I am always learning and will never claim to be infallible, to have all of the answers, or to be above feeling discomfort when I am challenged by someone or something. Remembering I am human helps me forgive white-bodied folks when it is possible for me to do so and to forgive myself for not being perfect as I navigate my own human experience.

In addition to remembering my own humanness and my lack of perfection, it's been important for me also to reflect on what accountability looks like as I work across lines of difference and to remember my vision for collective liberation. As we do our work, whether in or out of BIPOC-only spaces, it is important to think about what accountability looks like to one another and to vision for freedom for all BIPOC people. If we are working with white-bodied individuals and communities, it feels important for us to think about what accountability looks like across lines of difference as we each hold our vision for collective liberation for all and recognize we have different roles to play and different work to do.

Accountability

Accountability is a topic many folks in justice and organizing circles are talking about right now. It feels like a hot topic many are trying to figure out. Recently I was facilitating a workshop in a racially mixed space about yoga and social justice. I shared the group agreements with the attendees, community-care practices that are similar to the ones outlined in chapter 5. After I shared the agreements, a workshop attendee who was BIPOC asked me what accountability to the agreements looked like and what I do in groups when it seems as if people aren't being accountable to agreements.

This question made me curious about the group and its dynamics, about what had happened prior to my popping in there to offer a module in their much longer training course. It made me curious about what had already happened across lines of difference in the space. When the person asked me about accountability, it felt as if they were seeking a brave space where people could make mistakes and be accountable to one another—a space or container that was capable of holding our very messy humanness; a space that is able to call people to account for the harm they may have caused based on race or some other point of privilege, and a space made up of people who have taken time to consider what conditions need to be in place for repair to be possible.

I am still learning about accountability and what it means to build accountability in relationships. The system of criminal justice and the lynch-mob mentality have conditioned me to be punitive in my attempts to build accountability. This has never sat well with me because relationship and humanity aren't centered when we are punishing someone. Often what is centered is stripping someone of their humanity and shaming them into being a different way, which in my experience isn't an effective strategy for long-term personal or systemic transformation.

Throughout my time as an organizer and facilitator, I have witnessed people punish folks for not being woke enough, as if we all know everything we need to know and are awakened to all the ways suffering exists on the planet. I have witnessed a complete inability to extend grace, even though we all make mistakes. I have witnessed people cancel other people's humanity on social media. I have witnessed folks being threatened, as if healing can happen from a threat. It cannot. In the collectives of which I have been a part, I have also experienced diverse groups of people working through really challenging moments by going back to the agreements, taking a moment to pause, or calling people in to make amends and take responsibility for the actions that caused harm to an individual or multiple members of the group. I have seen groups move through restorative justice and community accountability processes toward the goal of healing and collective liberation.

> "What if we cherished opportunities to take accountability as precious opportunities to practice liberation? To practice love? To practice the kinds of people, elders-to-be, and souls we want to be? To practice that which we can only practice in real time? After all, we can only practice courage when we are afraid. We can only practice taking accountability when we have wronged or harmed or hurt. Practice yields the sharpest analysis."
>
> —MIA MINGUS, "Dreaming Accountability," *Leaving Evidence* (blog), May 5, 2019, https://leavingevidence.wordpress.com

As you engage the work of facilitating BIPOC affinity groups, and perhaps engage in dismantling racism and racial equity work, and as you consider accountability, reflect on the following:

REFLECTION QUESTIONS

- Where do you see opportunities to take and practice accountability as a practice of liberation?
- What does love have to do with accountability?
- As you do this work, what kind of person, elder, or elder-to-be or soul do you want to be?

If you choose to work across lines of difference in biracial training teams or as space-holders in a racial equity process that includes affinity groups, consider the skills and qualities that feel important to you for a white-bodied co-facilitator or space-holder to embody. Have many conversations with your white-bodied co-facilitator(s) about what you need from them when certain scenarios arise. Make sure they have some understanding of the extra burden you are carrying as a BIPOC person in a white supremacy culture, and as a BIPOC person holding a space for transformation to take place that is deeply tied to us as BIPOC people freeing ourselves from the patterns of behavior and trauma that manifest from racial trauma and internalized racial oppression while white-bodied individuals work to free themselves from internalized superiority and toxic patterns that emerge from the white supremacy culture. Some of these questions and conversations seem important to have with anyone you are working with, but especially if you are working in relationship with white-bodied individuals.

If we choose to work across racial lines of difference to take collective action, we need to be able to articulate what we need from white-bodied folks. We need white-bodied individuals to show up and be willing to commit to being accomplices and co-conspirators, concepts I explore in the next section of this chapter. We do not need more allies; we need white-bodied folks to be in continual inquiry with themselves and each other about what they are willing to risk for our liberation. We need to articulate what true solidarity would look like for us.

As you think about accountability and what is needed in relationship across racialized lines of difference, and how we take collective action in solidarity with one another, it is also important to consider the different roles we can play in supporting other BIPOC folks as well as thinking about how white-bodied individuals can support us.

Ally, Accomplice, Co-Conspirator

When I first began leading dismantling racism trainings, the term "ally" was thrown around as the archetype that white-bodied individuals should aspire to if they were in support of racial justice and liberation for BIPOC people. At that time, being an ally seemed to mean that someone who was more proximal to power based on their embodied identities would express an understanding of someone or a group of people less proximal to power, knowing they could not fully understand what that person or group of people's experience of oppression was like. Allyship simply meant one was supportive of a cause, but it didn't mean one would put anything on the line for justice.

Over time the language about right role in response to injustice has evolved and there is now more nuance and clarity about what is needed for us to upend systems of oppression like racism. The terms I hear used most often in conversations about collective action and solidarity are "accomplice" and "co-conspirator"; sometimes "comrade" is used for a co-conspirator. Each one of these archetypes suggests someone who is benefiting from your oppression within an oppressive system who is also willing to do something other than simply say they support a cause. In some way they are willing to fight the injustice you are facing in solidarity with you and they are willing to risk more—be that resources, emotional energy, or something physical—than you.

> "Accomplices actively work to dismantle systems of oppression. They have passed through the initial phase of allyship and done the requisite work of learning and understanding their roles in upholding unjust structures. Accomplices flip the dynamic and use what they've learned and whatever access they have to help course correct systemic bias."
>
> —DR. TIFFANY JANA, "The Differences Between Allies, Accomplices & Co-Conspirators May Surprise You," aninjusticemag.com, February 28, 2021
>
> "Co-conspiracy is about what we do in action, not just in language. It is about moving through guilt and shame and recognizing that we did not create none of this stuff. And so what we are taking responsibility for is the power that we hold to transform our conditions."
>
> —ALICIA GARZA, "Ally or Co-Conspirator?"
> Move to End Violence (website), September 7, 2016
>
> "A co-conspirator says, 'I know the terms; I know what white privilege and white supremacy mean; now, what risks am I willing to take?' It's saying, 'I'm going to put my privilege on the line for somebody.'"
>
> —DR. BETTINA LOVE, quoted in *To All the White Allies Seeking to Become Co-Conspirators, Here Are Things to Think About*, by Kim Smith

To be in right relationship and work with each other to take collective action in solidarity with other BIPOC people, we need to assess our points of oppression and privilege and ask what we are willing to risk for each other. What might it look like to be a co-conspirator or accomplice to other BIPOC people who are less proximal to power?

It might look like this: I was leading a workshop in a racially mixed BI-POC affinity group, and a woman of color apologized to another woman of color because she believed she had contributed to the woman who was less proximal to power being silent in the racially mixed group when we were all together. Healing happened in that moment. We must work to be aware of our points of privilege and proximity to power to truly be in solidarity with people, especially other BIPOC people who experience more marginalization than we do.

Celesté shares about the practice of holding the ways in which we, BIPOC people, are all affected by racism and the reality that the way we experience racism is different, depending on our racial identity.

When I was part of a nonprofit organizing team here in Colorado, we used to have quarterly trainings for our members. And one of the things that I helped to put together was a Know Your Rights Training that was broken out into affinity groups. There was a Black group, a Latinx group, and there was a white group. We did the Know Your Rights Training in those separate groups and spent the majority of our time in those affinity groups. But at the end of the Black and Latinx groups, they came together, and we had a shared conversation. I remember how powerful that was because there was adequate space for the people that were in the room, some of whom were immigrants and who were undocumented, to speak to their fears, their trauma, and for our Black leaders to speak to the racial profiling, fear, and oppression that they faced because of police.

We talked about how their experiences were not synonymous, but there were similarities. It helped our members to come to a place where they could actually be in greater solidarity and understand the systemic oppression that was happening. It's not just I.C.E. over here and police over there, but it's both systems oppressing us and harming our communities simultaneously. If I remember correctly, after that session, there were some requests made from the groups to each other, so that helped to build ongoing connection and dialogue.

—CELESTÉ MARTINEZ

Even though *A Space for Us* is focused on race, and in particular on facilitating BIPOC affinity groups, it also feels important to mention that if we are working across other lines of difference, we need to be in constant inquiry about who has less power in the space and to be asking ourselves what is my right role now? How can I be in right relationship with those who are less proximal to power? What do I need to learn? Do I need to move back and listen? Do I need to lean in? These questions and my own willingness to contemplate my right role based on the context and what is being called for at a particular point in time can bring me back to my values, vision, and intention to create a world in which everyone can be free.

And if we want to talk about beloved community, all being in relationship with one another and being in right relationship with each other, it is a multiracial, multi-identity coalition pushing for collective action. And we have to practice. We have to practice the future that we want to see.

—STEPHANIE GHOSTON PAUL

Stephanie is right. If you have any desire to build beloved community and coalitions across difference, we must practice if we want collective action and change. (The appendix includes a resource list with information about coalitions and beloved communities that are organizing and taking collective action together.)

Taking collective action does require us to do as Ruby Sales instructs: change ourselves. We must be able to challenge and change those things that are outside of who we truly are. The system of white supremacy created by white-bodied people is what split us apart on many levels and in many ways. Yet who we truly are is interconnected. By this I mean actively holding a vision for collective liberation and care and taking action based on the absolute truth that we are interconnected.

> "No one who has ever touched liberation could possibly want anything other than liberation for everyone."
> —REV. ANGEL KYODO WILLIAMS, "Your Liberation Is on the Line," *Lion's Roar: Buddhist Wisdom for Our Time*, February 2, 2020

CLOSING THOUGHTS

As I wrote *A Space for Us*, I was continually reminded of the importance of affinity groups. They are indeed a harm reduction and healing tool. While I knew I had much to say about facilitating BIPOC affinity groups, I had no idea I had so much to say about how to hold space for and with one another. Being a facilitator isn't a small job, especially when we are facilitating transformative healing justice work, which is exactly what we are doing as facilitators of affinity spaces. My hope is that through this book, you have learned more about yourself, your racial identity, how to hold space, the importance of affinity groups, and collective liberation. I long for a world in which our BIPOC bodies aren't used as targets or weapons. I long for a world in which we all have what we need and where we don't tear each other down as white supremacy works to tear us apart. I long for a world in which white-bodied individuals and communities risk everything to dismantle white supremacy and a world where we, as BIPOC people, can spend our time dreaming, resting, deep belly-laughing, singing, rejoicing, and sharing together in circle and ceremony. I believe in us, and as a facilitator of many groups, including BIPOC affinity groups, I believe in the power of what we can do as we hold space for and with one another.

May we all be free.
May we all find peace.
May we all heal.
May there always be a space for us.
Asé.
And so it is.
It is so.

APPENDIX

THERE ARE MANY resources available if you are interested in learning more about systemic racism and internalized oppression. In this appendix I focus on practices and sample agendas you can use in your facilitation of BIPOC affinity groups. I also include a brief list of books, articles, and podcasts that focus on anti-racism work.

SAMPLE AGENDAS

SAMPLE AGENDA #1 *Racialized Trauma and Ancestral Resilience*

SESSION LENGTH: 90 minutes

OPENING MEDITATION/CENTERING: 10 minutes

Offer a moment for people to come into the space, take a few deep breaths, and take some time to presence themselves.

CALLING OURSELVES INTO THE SPACE: 20 minutes

Invite folks to take a moment to surface a feeling that is present for them. Go around the room and invite each person to share their name, pronouns, and a feeling that is present for them.

ASSUMPTIONS/AGREEMENTS: 10 to 15 minutes

Share your list of assumptions and agreements or community-care practices.

CONTENT: 30 minutes

Define racial trauma—offer a definition of racial trauma and invite people to reflect on any signs or symptoms of racial trauma they experience.

Invite folks to share in small groups or the large group and note any themes that emerge within the group related to how racial trauma manifests for participants in the affinity group.

After you have shared back themes with the group, lead a body-centered practice from chapter 7 or one that you have found helpful in releasing energy or trauma.

ANCESTRAL RESILIENCE: Now invite folks to think of a healthy or well ancestor who embodied a resilient spirit despite the racialized trauma they experienced. This ancestor could be living or deceased. If it is difficult for a group participant to think of an ancestor, they can think of a mentor, guide, or teacher.

Have them take some time to reflect on gifts they received or lessons learned from this ancestor, guide, or mentor.

Invite people to move into small groups of three or four to share stories about the ancestor, guide, or mentor and then bring the group back together.

CLOSING: 15 minutes

Have participants go around the circle and share the ancestor, guide, or teacher's name along with a word or sentence that is representative of the gifts they received or lessons they learned from this ancestor, guide, or teacher.

Take time to sit in silence for a few minutes after everyone has shared.

SAMPLE AGENDA #2 *Processing Racialized Trauma*

SESSION LENGTH: 90 minutes

OPENING MEDITATION/CENTERING: 5 minutes

Offer a grounding meditation and invite participants to take a few deep breaths together. If you would like to offer an affirmation for them to work with, you might share something like "Breathing in, breathing out" or "I've arrived. I'm here."

You could also invite them to come up with their own affirmation and repeat it to themselves three times.

CALLING OURSELVES INTO THE SPACE: 10 minutes

Invite group participants to think of a color that is representative of how they feel. Go around the room and invite each person to share their name, pronouns, and the color that came into their awareness when prompted to think of a color representative of how they currently are feeling.

ASSUMPTIONS/AGREEMENTS: 10 to 15 minutes

Share your list of assumptions and agreements or community-care practices.

CONTENT: 50 minutes

Define racial trauma.

Have folks share a recent experience of racism. On a scale from 0 to 10, with 0 being no activation of the nervous system and 10 being over-activated, invite them to think of something that is a 5 or less.

Explain that they will move into small groups of three. In these groups, each person will have an opportunity to share for 5 minutes about their experience. Once the first person has shared, participants will have 7 minutes to ask open-ended questions such as these:

> What resources did you need at the time of the incident?
>
> How did you take care of yourself at the moment?
>
> How did you return to your body after your nervous system felt activated?
>
> If others had been around, what do you wish they would have done to support you?
>
> What kind of care do you now need?

After the period of open-ended questions, the person who shared and responded to the questions will have another three minutes to share anything else they want to about the incident or how they are feeling. Then the group will switch to someone else so they can share about their experience of racism or racial trauma.

This process will take about 15 minutes for each person in the group, a total of 45 minutes for each group.

CLOSING: 15 minutes

Invite the group to move through a body-centered practice and to go around the circle one more time to share an appreciation for the process of sharing stories, listening, being a witness and being witnessed by others, and being asked or asking open-ended questions.

SAMPLE AGENDA #3 *Internalized Racial Oppression*

SESSION LENGTH: 90 minutes

OPENING MEDITATION/CENTERING: 5 minutes

Offer a moment for people to come into the space, take a few deep breaths, and take some time to presence themselves.

CALLING OURSELVES INTO THE SPACE: 10 minutes

Invite folks to take a moment to surface a feeling that is present for them. Go around the room and invite each person to share their name, pronouns, and a feeling that is present for them.

ASSUMPTIONS/AGREEMENTS: 10 to 15 minutes

Share your list of assumptions and agreements or community-care practices.

CONTENT: 15 minutes

Define internalized oppression and have the group participants reflect on what manifests for them physically, emotionally, mentally, psychically, and spiritually in response to the negative messages they have internalized from the white supremacy culture about what it means to be Black, Indigenous, or a Person of Color. They can reflect by means of journaling, meditation, drawing, movement, or in some other way.

Once they have reflected on the prompt about internalized oppression, please ask each individual to reflect on the following prompt, offered to me by my friend Tiya Caniel:

If you were not limited by constructs, your body or mind, who would you be?

Once again, they may choose to reflect by journaling, meditating, or drawing, or through some embodied practice.

SMALL-GROUP DISCUSSION: 15 minutes

Put people in small groups and invite them to share about who they would be without constructs, a body, or mind.

LARGE-GROUP DISCUSSION: 15 minutes

When folks come back to the large group, invite them to share any reflections, observations, or feelings from their small group discussions.

Invite the group as a whole to reflect on the reality that they have internalized negative messages and that we are all much more than the messages we are being told about ourselves.

CLOSING: 20 minutes

End this group with a practice of rest and dreaming. Invite folks to find a comfortable posture and to return to the prompt about who they would be if they weren't limited by constructs, a body, or mind. Invite them to breathe and sit and dream about this vision and version of themselves. Allow them to be in this process for at least 5 minutes.

Close with a go-around where each participant shares a feeling word.

If you only have an hour or 75 minutes, you can adapt the introductions and content. Please make sure to mindfully open and close the group.

BODY-SCAN SCRIPTS

I include here two additional body-scan scripts in addition to those offered in chapter 7.

Script #1

Take a moment to find a posture. If possible, a comfortable posture. You can sit, lie down, or stand. If you have chosen to sit on the ground, you might want some support from a pillow or blanket. You can sit on the pillow or blanket to provide your spine and body with more support. Rest your hands wherever they feel most comfortable. People often place their hands on their knees, palms faceup or facedown.

Take a moment to tune into your breath and heartbeat.

As you breathe, notice the sensations in your body. Take a moment to scan your entire body and notice what sensations are present at this time.

Begin to cultivate an attitude of curiosity in response to what you notice.

Place one hand on your heart and one on your belly, and notice the quality of your breath: is it smooth or jagged, long or slow? Are your inhalations and exhalations even in length? Where does the breath first enter the body? Does the breath lift the hand on the belly at all? There is no need to change anything. Right now, you are becoming aware of the breath and how it moves through your body.

Now, with each breath feel yourself becoming more rooted and connected to the earth. If you would like to tense the muscles in the lower body, take a moment to tense and release them. You can repeat this a few times.

Now, tense the muscles in the middle of your body, your belly, glutes, and low back, and release them. You can repeat this a few times.

You can move to the upper body, arms, neck, and face, tensing your muscles and releasing them a few times.

Now the entire body. Squeeze or tense the entire body and hold for a few seconds, and then release. Repeat this a few times.

Now take a few deep breaths, breathe consciously, and notice how your body feels. (Allow at least two minutes of this deep conscious breathing.)

I invite you to take a moment to offer an affirmation of gratitude. You might say something like "I am grateful to be here today," or "I am grateful for my breath," or "I am grateful for all I have in my life." Repeat this affirmation three times and notice how your heart feels.

Take a few more deep breaths here and gently return to the space. Take some time to reorient in your space, noticing what is around you—colors, shapes, light, and living beings.

Script #2

Begin by finding a comfortable posture.

Bring your attention to your breath and take a few deep breaths.

I now invite you to bring your attention to your entire body.

You can notice your body seated wherever you're seated, feeling the weight of your body on the chair, on the floor.

Take a few deep breaths.

And as you take a deep breath, bring in more oxygen, and as you exhale, release the breath and relax more deeply.

Bring your awareness to the back part of your body and take a moment to connect with all of the well ancestors who came before you. Feel their support behind you. Bring your awareness to your feet or whatever parts of the body are touching or close to the ground. Deepen your connection with the earth and feel the support of the ground and earth.

Bring your attention to your stomach area. If you notice tension in your stomach, practice letting your stomach soften.

Take a deep breath.

Notice your hands. If you sense tightness in your hands, see if you can soften them.

Notice your arms. Feel the sensations present as you notice your arms.

Take a deep breath and relax your arms and shoulders more fully.

Now notice your neck and throat. Let them be soft. Relax.

Soften your jaw.

Soften your brow.

Soften your face.

Now notice your whole body present.

Take five deep breaths.

Be aware of your whole body as best you can.

Take a deep breath.

When you feel ready, gently return to the space.

The following are supplemental activities you can use as you facilitate affinity groups. They are meant to deepen connections among affinity group participants and to support affinity group participants in being present as to how they are feeling and to feel affirmed in their being.

SUPPLEMENTAL ACTIVITIES

Meditation for Connection

Begin by finding a comfortable posture.

Bring your attention to your breath and take a few deep breaths.

I invite you to bring your attention to your body.

You can notice your body seated wherever you're seated, feeling the weight of your body on the chair, on the floor.

Take a few deep breaths.

And as you take a deep breath, bring in more oxygen, and as you exhale, release the breath and relax more deeply.

Bring your awareness to the back part of your body and take a moment to connect with all of the well ancestors who came before you. Feel their support behind you. Bring your awareness to your feet or whatever parts of the body are touching or close to the ground. Deepen your connection with the earth and feel the support of the ground and earth.

Bring your awareness to the sides of your body and feel support on both sides of you.

Bring your awareness to the crown of your head, feeling support from the celestial realm and the cosmos. Feel support from the great mystery, void, darkness, and your higher self.

Take a few breaths to feel support from behind, below, above, and around you.

Stay here for as long as you would like, and when you feel ready, return to your space.

Mindful Observation

Take a moment to find an object in the space that doesn't carry an emotional charge or an object that brings you joy. Take some time to connect with this object and notice everything you can about it—the colors, words or letters on it, its texture, and so on. Gaze at this object for about two minutes, allowing yourself to connect with its energy and to feel the neutrality or joy it brings to you. When you feel ready, break your gaze on this object and take a few deep breaths.

The Oracles

If you are meeting in person with the affinity group, have some index cards on hand. At the opening or closing of the group, hand out the cards and invite folks to write an affirmation on their card. Place the cards in a hat or vessel. Send the vessel around the group and have folks pick one card out of it. Have them take a moment to silently read their affirmation. Then invite everyone to go around the circle and speak their affirmation into the space. If you have time, you can break into small groups and invite participants to share their affirmation (the one they received) and something about why they believe they chose that affirmation.

Box Breathing

Box breathing has been shown to decrease anxiety and calm the nervous system.

Begin by inviting the group participants to find a comfortable way to be and let them know you will lead a breathing activity. Invite them to breathe naturally, to begin with their natural inhaling and exhaling, for one to two minutes. Then invite folks to breathe in for a count of four. At the top of their inhale invite them to hold their breath for four seconds, then exhale for a count of four. Invite the group to repeat these steps for at least two minutes.

INTERVIEWEES

I interviewed several amazing and brilliant people for *A Space for Us*. Here I tell you more about their biographies and work and how to connect with them through their websites.

Stephanie Ghoston Paul

Stephanie Ghoston Paul (she/her) is a purpose-whisperer, ecosystem con-
nector, and culture alchemist. Her work in the world is all about identity
and remembering to re-member. In the context of individuals, that looks
like self-care and boundaries work to help leaders balance their lives by
coming back to themselves. In the community context, Stephanie holds
space for collective healing through truth telling and explores what it
means to be a living ancestor. In the organizational context, that looks like
naming harm, imagining liberatory ways of being, and engaging in the
messy culture and people work needed for that transformation. Stephanie
believes that when people, communities, and ecosystems get in alignment
with and fully embody their purpose, we move toward a future where all
human beings are free, whole, and enough.

Stephanie is also a best-selling author, podcast host, documentarian,
and recent TEDx speaker. She centers ease and care in her life and her
work, making sure to practice what she preaches. When she's not working
Stephanie enjoys cooking spicy dishes with her partner, finding new flavors
of delicious tea, and witnessing her toddler discover the world.

WEBSITE: www.stephanieghoston.com

Lisa Anderson

Lisa Anderson is vice president for embodied justice leadership at Auburn Seminary, where she works with Auburn's program team to advance
multifaith movements for justice by creating spaces where faith- and
spirit-rooted leaders engage in intersectional organizing, bridging the
divide between theology and activism, and equipping and deepening the
spiritual grounding of leaders in a multifaith movement for justice via the
creation and curation of worship and liturgical resources.

Lisa is also founding director of the Sojourner Truth Leadership Circle, a fellowship program whose mission is to make the ordinary care of
the bodies, minds, and spirits of Black and Brown women a priority in their
own lives and within the social justice spaces where Black women leaders
disproportionately serve. It also equips Black and Brown women leaders
who are seeking to advance movements for justice within their communities, through a methodology that incorporates a vigorous and spiritually
grounded practice of self-care as a part of a leader's public witness.

Before coming to Auburn, Lisa designed seminars on national and international affairs through the General Board of Global Ministries of the United Methodist Church. There she helped lay leaders connect their professions of Christian faith to concrete and spiritually grounded activism for social change and transformation. Lisa was also a leader and facilitator at Marble Collegiate Church, working specifically on behalf of the Women's Ministry, Young Adult Ministry, and the Senior Fellowship. Lisa has worked on issues of food justice and as an advocate for poor women and children through the United Way–sponsored Dutchess Outreach in Dutchess County, New York, where she supervised a volunteer staff of over one hundred.

Lisa is a graduate of Vassar College and holds master of divinity and master of philosophy degrees from Union Theological Seminary. She has taught courses in Black, womanist, feminist, and LGBTQ theologies, ethics, and liturgy. She is a regular contributor to several blogs and journals, including the journal *Theology & Sexuality*, and contributed to the book *Women, Spirituality, and Transformative Leadership*.

Jeanine T. Abraham

Jeanine T. Abraham is a writer, an actor, an entertainment and wellness journalist, a movement-based theater artist, a storyteller, a GirlTrek faculty member, a self-taught chef, and a yoga student with twenty-five years of practice.

WEBSITE: www.visableblackwoman.com

Celesté Martinez

Celesté Martinez is a queer Chicana born in Santa Cruz, California, and raised in San Antonio, Texas, who has called Denver, Colorado, home for over a decade. Politically active in her Colorado community, she identifies as Chicana while embracing the complexity of being a mestiza of Indigenous Cherokee and Mexica lineages as well as of Spanish descent.

Her experience—from working as a community organizer to director of a nonprofit—has taught Celesté invaluable lessons, which she often calls upon to translate her diverse skill set to meet the needs of her individual and organizational clients through her business, Celestial Alegria. Through Celestial Alegria, Celesté is committed to igniting joy through transformation through her array of services, which include life coaching, facilitation, and racial equity consulting. She also offers annual community programs known as the Confronting Anti-Blackness for Latinx & Chicanx and the Reparations Network.

You can most commonly find her making music through her solo project, Soy Celesté, writing poetry, hanging at community events, and loving on her two Chihuahua pups.

WEBSITE: celestialalegria.com

Natasha Harrison

An Atlanta native, Natasha A. Harrison is a wife, a mother, a philanthropist, a community advocate, and an entrepreneur. She shares her personal story—from Washington, DC, to Atlanta—of endurance and resilience to motivate others to give their time, talent, and treasure.

By the time Natasha was eight years old, a family friend had sexually abused her. She witnessed her mother being physically abused by her alcoholic stepfather, and on occasion was a victim of the same abuse. By the time she was eighteen, she had moved fourteen times in twelve years and had assumed legal guardianship of her nine-year-old brother after her mother died of heart valve failure three days after her high school graduation.

In 2011, she founded CommunityBuild Ventures, a strategic solutions firm committed to providing coaching, training, and consultation to non-profits, businesses, and government agencies to assist them with defining strategic solutions that address issues in African American communities. Some notable clients of her firm are Gas South, the Annie E. Casey Foundation, the Capital One Foundation, the DC Trust for Youth, and the DC Department of Youth Rehabilitation Services.

In addition to her role as president and CEO at CommunityBuild Ventures, Natasha is an adjunct professor at Georgia State University's Andrew Young School of Policy Studies and a frequent facilitator and lecturer at the Georgia Center for Nonprofits.

Natasha is a member of HouseProud Atlanta's board of directors, a member of Circle of Joy Giving Circle, the founder of For Her: A Black Women Giving Movement for Black Girls, a member of the Ryan Cameron Foundation Anti-Violence Taskforce, a co-chair of the twelfth annual Community Investment Network Conference, a cabinet member of United Way Women of Cole, and a member of the Junior League of

Atlanta. She was selected the EnVest Foundation 40 under 40 honoree due to her outstanding service to her community.

She is a devoted wife to Ayodele Harrison and mother to Ajani and Ifetayo.

WEBSITES: http://breakthesilo.com; https://communitybuildventures.com

Ayodele Harrison

Ayodele Harrison is a transportation engineer turned master math educator and educational consultant. From Oakland, California, to Washington, DC, to Johannesburg, South Africa, Ayodele has been a math educator and has assumed a wide range of roles to support school and student access for more than fifteen years. He has taught in public, private, and international school communities. Additionally, Ayodele has designed, facilitated, and directed STEM-focused learning activities and camps for girls, children of color, and other vulnerable youth.

Ayodele is senior partner with the Atlanta-based firm Community-Build Ventures. He believes that in the right learning environment, all educators view their work in schools as worthwhile and fulfilling and all youths are positioned to excel academically and thrive individually. That said, he invests his time, talents, and treasures in equipping K–20 educators with strategies and tools to "get the environment right." He provides research-guided and classroom-tested professional development solutions for educators and schools in the form of trainings, coaching, and consulting.

Since 2015, Ayodele has facilitated workshops and learning sessions throughout the Southeast for over five hundred K–20 educators and community leaders under the auspices of numerous organizations such as the National Association of Independent Schools, the Martin Institute for Teaching Excellence at Georgia State University, and the Georgia Council of Teachers of Mathematics.

Born in Seattle, Ayodele holds both bachelor's and master's of science degrees in civil engineering, from Howard University and the University of California, Berkeley, respectively. He lives in Atlanta with his wife, Natasha, and two children, Ajani and Ifetayo.

WEBSITE: http://ayodeleharrison.com

Sherene Cauley

Sherene Cauley (she/her) is a National Board Certified Health and Wellness Coach, the founder of the Nurtured Life, and the associate director of the Whole Health Center in Bar Harbor, Maine. She is working toward her doctor of ministry degree with a focus on social transformation at United Theological Seminary of the Twin Cities.

Sherene lives with her husband, mother, and children on the coast of Maine. As someone who has struggled throughout her life with dyslexia, she began to recognize how her many neurodivergent sensitivities help her to tune in to her internal and external environments, which allows her not only to experience her spirituality more fully but also to guide others in healing practices that are responsive to mind and body. The Nurtured Life has evolved as a wellness coaching service for clients across the country and includes workshops on attuning to our inner and outer realities to build supportive, sustainable lifestyles.

Sherene's academic research has examined the effects of hegemonic white patriarchy on spirituality and human development. As an American and woman of Iranian heritage, she recognized both socially and personally the harm caused by racial structures and the need to actively cultivate a culture of well-being. She continues to combine her knowledge in health coaching, peace studies, and wisdom traditions to offer coaching around barriers to peace, equity, and social justice.

WEBSITE: thenurturedlife.org

ADDITIONAL RESOURCES

Online Resources

Calling Out vs Calling In White Supremacy Culture, https://creative equitytoolkit.org/topic/anti-racism/call-out-call-in-racism

Dismantling Racism Works (dRworks), https://www.dismantling racism.org

National Museum of African American History and Culture (Smithsonian Institution), Being Anti Racist (website), https://nmaahc.si.edu /learn/talking-about-race/topics/being-antiracist

National Seeking Educational Equity and Diversity (SEED) Project, resources and standard pedagogy, https://nationalseedproject.org

Native Land Information System, native-land.ca

Racial Equity Institute, https://www.racialequityinstitute.com

Racial Equity Tools, https://www.racialequityinstitute.com

Western States Center, https://www.westernstatescenter.org

White Supremacy Culture, https://www.whitesupremacyculture.info

Books

Alexander, Michelle. *The New Jim Crow: Mass Incarceration in the Age of Colorblindness*. New York: New Press, 2010.

Birdsong, Mia. *How We Show Up: Reclaiming Family, Friendship, and Community*. New York: Hachette Go, 2020.

Brown, Adrienne Maree. *Emergent Strategy*. Chico, CA: AK Press, 2017.

Channing, Austin. *I'm Still Here: Black Dignity in a White World*. New York: Random House/Convergent Books, 2018.

Cullors, Patrisse. *An Abolitionist's Handbook: 12 Steps to Changing Yourself and the World*. New York: St. Martin's Press, 2021.

Kaba, Mariame. *We Do This 'Til We Free Us: Abolitionist Organizing and Transforming Justice (Abolitionist Papers)*. Chicago: Haymarket Books, 2021.

Kendi, Ibram X. *How to Be an Anti-Racist*. New York: Penguin Random House, 2019.

King, Ruth. *Mindful Race*. N.p.: Sounds True One (https://join.sounds true.com), 2018.

Magee, Rhonda V. *The Inner Work of Racial Justice: Healing Ourselves and Transforming Our Communities Through Mindfulness*. New York: TarcherPerigee, 2019.

Menakem, Resmaa. *My Grandmother's Hands: Racialized Trauma and the Pathway to Mending Our Hearts and Bodies*. Las Vegas: Central Recovery Press, 2017.

Oluo, Ijeoma. *So You Wanna Talk About Race*. New York: Basic Books, 2018.

Ortiz, Roxanne. *An Indigenous Peoples' History of the United States*. Boston: Beacon Press, 2015.

Owens, Lama Rod. *Love and Rage: The Path of Liberation Through Anger*. Berkeley, CA: North Atlantic Books, 2020.

Parker, Gail. *Restorative Yoga for Ethnic and Race-Based Stress and Trauma*. Philadelphia: Singing Dragon, 2020.

Raheem, Octavia. *Gather*. Independently published, 2020.

Raheem, Octavia. *Pause, Rest, Be: Stillness Practice for Courage in Times of Change*. Boston: Shambhala, 2022.

Saad, Layla. *Me and White Supremacy: Combat Racism, Change the World, and Become a Good Ancestor*. Chicago: Sourcebooks, 2020.

Singh, Anneliese. *The Racial Healing Handbook: Practical Activities to Help You Challenge Privilege, Confront Systemic Racism, and Engage in Collective Healing*. Oakland, CA: New Harbinger Publications, 2019.

Taylor, Sonia Renee. *The Body Is Not an Apology*. Oakland, CA: Berrett-Koehler, 2018.

Wade, Breeshia. *Grieving While Black: An Antiracist Take on Oppression and Sorrow*. Berkeley, CA: North Atlantic Books, 2021.

Wilkerson, Isabel. *Caste: The Origins of Our Discontents*. New York: Random House, 2020.

Videos

Courageous Conversation. https://courageousconversation.com/courageous -conversations-about-race-a-field-guide-for-achieving-racial-equity -in-schools.

Eyes on the Prize. Documentary. Washington, DC: PBS, 1987.

Conversations on Race. Series of videos. *New York Times*, 2015 to present.

Race: The Power of an Illusion. Three-part documentary. San Francisco: California Newsreel, 2003.

13th. Feature-length documentary. Directed by Ava DuVernay, 2016.

Articles

Barkataki, Susanna. "Internalized Oppression: Healing Scars You Can't See." *Huffington Post*, April 5, 2016, https://www.huffingtonpost.com /susanna-barkataki/internalized-oppression-h_b_9617644.html.

Barkataki, Susanna. "10 Liberating Ways to Overcome Internalized Oppression." *Elephant Journal* (blog), April 6, 2016, https://www .elephantjournal.com/2015/04/10-liberating-ways-to-overcome -internalized-oppression.

Coates, Ta-Nehisi. "The Case for Reparations." *The Atlantic*, June 2014.

Drake, Sunny. "Racism Is to White People as Wind Is to Sky." July 14, 2013. Posted privately on https://sunnydrake.wordpress.com.

Jayakumar, Kirthi. "Intersectionality: A Primer." The Gender Security Project (website), January 22, 2020, https://www.gendersecurity project.com/post/intersectionality-a-primer.

McKenzie, Mia. "No More 'Allies.'" *Black Girl Dangerous* (blog), September 30, 2013.

Race Forward: The Center for Racial Justice Innovation. *Moving the Race Conversation Forward*. Report. New York: Race Forward, January 2014.

Podcasts

Code Switch, https://www.npr.org/podcasts/510312/codeswitch

CTZNWELL, https://www.ctznwell.org/ctznpodcast

The Good Ancestor, http://laylafsaad.com/good-ancestor-podcast

Healing Justice, https://irresistible.org/podcast

Speaking of Racism, https://speakingofracism.com

ACKNOWLEDGMENTS

FIRST AND FOREMOST, I want to acknowledge my ancestors. *A Space for Us* is a love letter to you all for bringing me into being. Thank you, ancestors, for moving words, medicine, dreams, and ideas, all in support of the collective good through me. Thank you to all those known and unknown ancestors whose blood flows through my veins and whose hearts beat through my heartbeat. Thank you to the ancestors who may not be well and healthy but who have allowed me to do this work to heal our bloodline. Thank you to the healthy and well ancestors; you have a plan that I trust is unfolding in good order. I trust you infinitely.

Thank you to my mother, Clara. The ancestors and Spirit knew what they were doing when they chose you to be my mother and me to be your daughter. I love you so much. Thank you for believing in me always and forever. Your bright light illuminates the entire cosmos, and your heart is one of the most beautiful hearts I have ever known. Mom, thank you for being here with us, on the planet, at this time. We need your heart, love, and light.

Thank you to the entire Dismantling Racism Collective. You most certainly inspired this book. Our collective has held a vision for collective liberation for all for so long. This vision has changed me, called me into doing the necessary and sometimes difficult work of truth-telling, and brought me into community with so many brilliant people who felt called to vision and create a world in which we all can be free. In particular, I want to thank Kenneth Jones and Cynthia Brown, two of my colleagues who co-wrote this book with me from above. Even though you both have transitioned from the earthly to heavenly realm, I felt you with me the entire time I wrote *A Space for Us*. In so many ways, you made a space for me. You mentored me—a deep bow of never-ending gratitude to you both.

Thank you to Vivette Jeffries-Logan, a dear friend and co-trainer for many years. Vivette, your medicine is contained in *A Space for Us*. Thank you for teaching me about the power of sitting in circles and just being with one another. No agenda. No goal. Thank you for teaching me how to sit in the space we as BIPOC so desperately need, a space that is dedicated to us and our healing.

Thank you to Tema Okun, Jonathan Henderson, Cristina Rivera, Keagha Carscallen, and Jes Kelly. We have walked on this path for so long; for me, being in so many spaces with you all as we led trainings, held What I Know for Sure gatherings, and had planning meetings for dRworks, has truly been a gift. You all are gifts, and I am so grateful to have been in deep community with you for so long.

Thank you to Stephanie, Sherene, Celesté, Natasha, Ayodele, Jeanine, and Lisa for allowing me to interview you and include your brilliance in *A Space for Us*. This book wouldn't be the same without your wisdom. Thank you for sharing it with me and us, and thank you for being. Your medicine and wisdom are needed at this time and as we create a space for ourselves to thrive and be free.

Thank you to Erin Trent-Johnson, who has inspired me in so many ways. Erin, thank you for sharing your magic in the foreword and for being on the path of liberation with me.

Thank you to Charles, my partner. It's no mistake that we had some issues specific to race come up in our relationship while I was writing *A Space for Us*. We've always known we were different. You are white. I am Black. And we are so much more than white and Black. The way we've navigated the situation with folks who may disapprove of our relationship has taught me a ton about grace, boundaries, love, and compassion. What we have waded through is reflective of what so many folks are wading through at this time—how to relate across difference. And while I wish the entire world would heal and learn to be better equipped at holding multiple truths and differences while striving for freedom for all, I believe the timing of the issues that arose in our relationship and my writing this book were synchronous. We had to practice holding our differences while we centered love. I am not sure we knew this is what we had signed up for when we met many moons ago, but I am grateful for the work and practice. I am thankful for you. For all you do to make life a bit easier for me. All you do to make me feel cared for and loved. Thank you for being you.

I have experienced countless circles that have felt sacred to me. Thank you to all the people who have sat in circle with me virtually or in person. Thank you for laughing, crying, questioning, sitting in silence, and creating a space for holy communion. Thank you for the part of the circle you are, and thanks for coming together in circle. Thank you for teaching me about your ceremonies and inviting us to merge our alchemy into a strong force that will most certainly serve the collective good.

Thank you to my best friend, Amy. You are my soul sister, and I dig you. So much. Thank you for being alive at this time. I am happy we get to be besties this go-around. I love you to the moon and back.

Thank you to Tristan Katz. Thank you for saying YES. Yes, to all of the new projects. Thank you for always celebrating me and what I birth, and thank you for the work you do in the world. Thank you for being my comrade and friend. I feel so grateful to be in community with you. I am grateful for your authenticity and integrity. I love you.

Thank you to Jasper. I am so very grateful to be in the world with you at this time. Thank you for protecting and loving me. Thank you for making me laugh. Thank you for cuddling with me and being the best writing partner I could ever ask for. Thank you for being my road dog. Jasper, we've been so many places, and I love that you are journeying with me in this lifetime. I love you.

NOTES

FOREWORD

1. Bettina Love, *We Want to Do More Than Survive: Abolitionist Teaching and the Pursuit of Educational Freedom* (Boston: Beacon Press, 2019).

CHAPTER 1: WHITE SUPREMACY, RACISM, AND THE FOUR FOUNDATIONS

1. Kimberlé Crenshaw, "Demarginalizing the Intersection of Race and Sex: A Black Feminist Critique of Antidiscrimination Doctrine, Feminist Theory and Antiracist Politics," *University of Chicago Legal Forum*, vol. 1989, art. 8 (1989), https://chicagounbound.uchicago.edu/uclf/vol1989/iss1/8.

2. Layla Saad, "Minimalism, Essentialism, and the Path of the Good Ancestor," *Letters from Layla*, Laylafsaad.com, February 1, 2021, http://laylafsaad.com /letters-from-layla/minimalism-essentialism-and-the-path-of-the-good-ancestor.

3. Charlotte Ruhl, "Implicit or Unconscious Bias," *Simply Psychology*, July 1, 2020, https://www.simplypsychology.org/implicit-bias.html.

4. "What Is Racism? Racism Defined," Dismantling Racism Works (dRworks), March 2022, https://www.dismantlingracism.org/racism-defined.html.

5. "What Is Racism? Racism Defined."

6. "What Is Racism? Racism Defined."

7. "Internalizations," dRworks, March 2022, https://www.dismantlingracism .org/racism-defined.html.

CHAPTER 2: A PLACE WHERE WE CAN BE

1. dRworks, *Dismantling Racism Works Web Workbook*, dRworksBook, 2013, https://www.dismantlingracism.org.

CHAPTER 3: EVERY CHILD'S TREASURE

1. Ann Cammett, "Deadbeat Dads & Welfare Queens: How Metaphor Shapes Poverty Law," *Boston College Journal of Law and Social Justice* 34, no. 2 (May 2014), art. 3.

2. Sarah-Soonling Blackburn, *What Is the Model Minority Myth?*, Learning for Justice (website), March 21, 2019, https://www.learningforjustice.org/magazine /what-is-the-model-minority-myth.

3. "Internalizations," dRworks, March 2022, https://www.dismantlingracism .org/internalizations.html.

4. "Internalizations," dRworks.

CHAPTER 4: ANTI-BLACKNESS AND THE MYTH OF RACE

1. Resmaa Menakem, *My Grandmother's Hands: Racialized Trauma and the Pathway to Mending Our Hearts and Bodies* (Las Vegas: Central Recovery Press, 2017).

2. "History of the Race Construct," dRworks, April 2022, https://www.dismantlingracism.org/history.html.

3. "History of the Race Construct."

4. "History of the Race Construct."

5. Jennie Lebowitz, "Muslim American Youth in the Post 9/11 Public Education System," American Cultural Studies Capstone Research Papers, Fairhaven College of Interdisciplinary Studies, Western Washington University, 2016.

6. Dismantling Racism Works, The History of the Race Construct [PowerPoint slides], 2020, https://drive.google.com/file/d/1zpGu3Ktcfdh-omP3mpPp2K9Q9P68GUon/view?usp=sharing.

7. Langston Hughes, *Selected Poems of Langston Hughes: A Classic Collection of Poems by a Master of American Verse* (New York: Vintage Classics, 1990).

CHAPTER 5: HOW WE BEGIN

1. Octavia Raheem, *Pause, Rest, Be: Stillness Practices for Courage in Times of Change* (Boulder, CO: Shambhala Publications, 2022).

CHAPTER 6: SKILLFUL FACILITATION

1. Thoth Adan, "Symbols Based on Circles," https://thoth-adan.com/blog/symbols-based-on-circles, accessed September 8, 2022.

2. Loretta Ross, "Loretta Ross on Calling In the Calling Out Culture," *Presidian Blog* (Presidio College), May 10, 2021, https://www.presidio.edu/blog/loretta-ross-on-calling-in-the-calling-out-culture.

CHAPTER 10: THE ROLE OF RITUALS

1. Tada Hozumi, "How Social Change Actually Happens: Through the Body," Tada Hozumi website, October 17, 2019, https://www.tadahozumi.org/how-change-actually-happens.

ABOUT THE AUTHOR

MICHELLE CASSANDRA JOHNSON is an author, spiritual teacher, social justice activist, intuitive healer, and dismantling racism educator. She approaches her life and work from a place of knowing we are, can, and must heal individually and collectively. Michelle teaches workshops and immersions, and leads retreats and transformative experiences nationwide. As a dismantling racism educator, she has worked with large corporations, nonprofits, and community groups. Michelle was a TEDx speaker at Wake Forest University in 2019 and has been interviewed on several podcasts in which she explores the premise and foundation of *Skill in Action*, along with embodied approaches to racial equity work, creating ritual in justice spaces, our divine connection with nature and Spirit, and how we as a culture can heal. Michelle published the first edition of *Skill in Action: Radicalizing Your Yoga Practice to Create a Just World* in 2017 and the second edition in 2021. Her second book, *Finding Refuge: Heart Work for Healing Collective Grief* was published in 2021. Her 2023 book, *We Heal Together: Rituals and Practice for Building Community and Connection*, explores the deep knowing and truth that we are interconnected; we belong to one another. *We Heal Together* offers rituals and practices meant to dream us into a new way of being to benefit the highest and fullest good.

She leads from the heart with courage, compassion, and a commitment to address the heartbreak that dominant culture causes for many because of the harm it creates. She inspires change that allows people to stand in their humanity and wholeness in a world that fragments most of us. Whether in an anti-oppression training, yoga space, individual or group intuitive healing session, the heart, healing, and wholeness are at the center of how she approaches all of her work in the world. Michelle can be found at www.michellecjohnson.com.